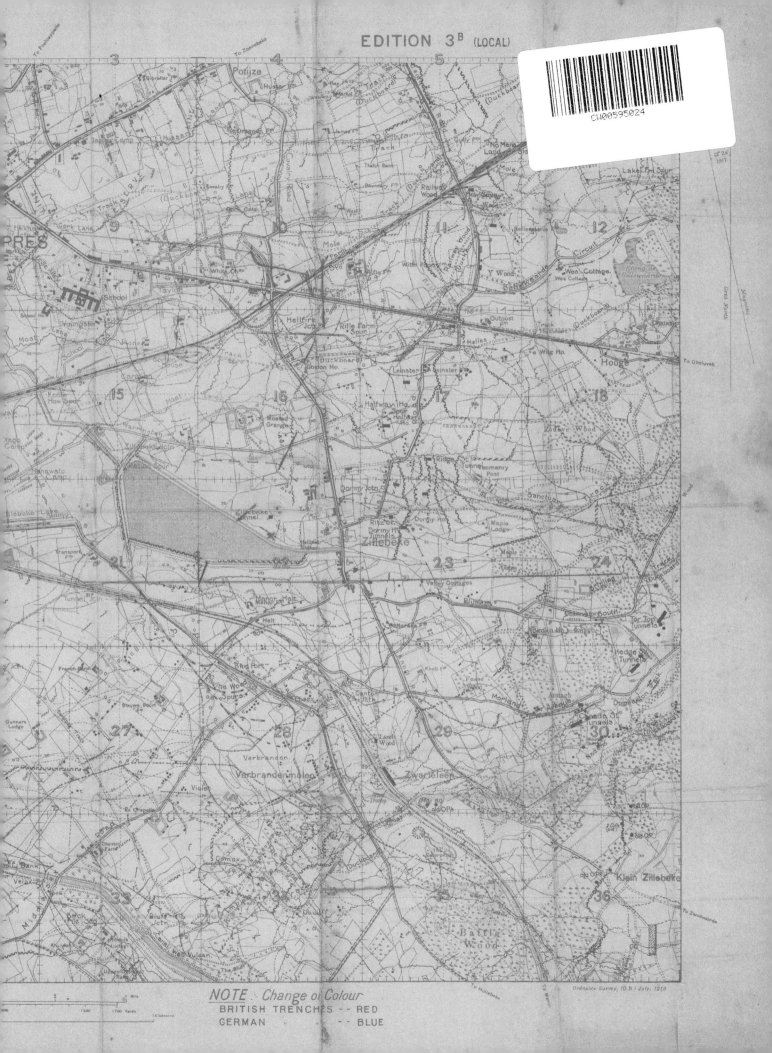

EDITION 3^B (LOCAL)

NOTE :- *Change of Colour*
BRITISH TRENCHES -- RED
GERMAN -- BLUE

THE
FRONTLINE
WALK

Edited by **Steve Roberts**
and **Terry Whenham**

THE
FRONTLINE
WALK

Following in the
footsteps of those who fought

UNIFORM

Nicole Duncan Tribute:

During the writing of this book, the sad news was received that one of the Frontline Walkers, Nicole Duncan, had died. Nicole took part in the 2017 and 2018 Frontline Walks, and was a very popular member of the team. Nicole's sister Megan spoke fondly of how: *"The Frontline Walk meant a lot to Nicole, both the history and friends she made, and she spoke about them often. It is an honour to know that she will be remembered by the charity that meant so much to her."*

Rest in peace, Nicole.

First published by Uniform
an imprint of Unicorn Publishing Group LLP, 2020
5 Newburgh Street
London W1F 7RG
www.unicornpublishing.org

10 9 8 7 6 5 4 3 2 1

ISBN 978-1-912690-78-7

Designed by Matthew Wilson
Printed by FineTone Ltd

THE
FRONTLINE
WALK

ABF
THE SOLDIERS'
CHARITY

The Army's National Charity
75TH ANNIVERSARY
1944–2019

CONTENTS

FOREWORD

Brigadier (Ret'd) Robin Bacon, Chief of Staff, ABF The Soldiers' Charity

In my capacity as Chief of Staff for ABF The Soldiers' Charity, I have had the privilege of representing the Charity at many of our events, getting to know our fantastic and loyal supporters. Since its inception in 2014, The Frontline Walk has been a highlight of my year and I always look forward to joining this special group of supporters as we walk through the historical French and Belgian countryside.

The walk first started as a commemoration event for the Centenary of the First World War. In our first year we had just 35 walkers, an amazing group of people who supported the Walk into its second year when it started to garner a following. It is down to everyone who has taken part each year that the Walk has been such a success and it is only fitting that their stories are told in the following pages. It is truly an honour for the Charity to have a book written about The Frontline Walk, and we are immensely grateful to the two authors.

We first met Steve Roberts in a bar in Arras during The Frontline Walk in 2014. We had just arrived in France for the very beginning of the first Frontline Walk and Steve was guiding another group, signalling himself out as a supporter with his charity wristband. This was the beginning of a great friendship, and soon enough as The Frontline Walk grew, we brought him on board as our historian. Now, he's become part of the furniture.

Terry Whenham was also with us on this inaugural Frontline Walk. He stuck with us through the trials and tribulations of a first-year event, with some questionable food choices, some rickety minibuses and a tremendously eclectic and colourful bunch of participants. Since then Terry has become a real stalwart of The Frontline Walk, acting as an 'official, unofficial' historian.

Underpinning The Frontline Walk and its fascinating history is the underlying cause that the Walk supports. The Soldiers' Charity depends on the support of the public taking part in events such as The Frontline Walk, to help us give practical and financial assistance to soldiers, veterans and their families in times of need.

2019 marked our 75th Anniversary. We have been the Army's National Charity since 1944, and thanks to the incredible generosity of our supporters, we will be helping hundreds of thousands of individuals and their families far into the future.

During the centenary years of the First World War, The Frontline Walk has raised over £1.25m for The Soldiers' Charity. This is an incredible achievement by our supporters and a worthy tribute to the men whose stories are told in this book.

Brigadier (Ret'd) Robin Bacon
Chief of Staff, ABF The Soldiers' Charity

INTRODUCTION

In 2019, ABF The Soldiers' Charity marked 75 years as the Army's national charity, having provided a lifetime of support for soldiers, veterans and their families since 1944. In its 75th year, it supported 70,000 people in 68 countries across the globe.

The Frontline Walk has been a vital part of that history, having generated over £1m since its inception in 2014. Looking to the future, the charity will continue to build on past successes to ensure that it remains the bedrock of charitable support to the Army family.

PART 1
Background

CHAPTER 1

WHY DOES THE ABF THE SOLDIERS' CHARITY EXIST?

The Soldiers' Charity gives a lifetime of support to soldiers and veterans from the British Army, and their immediate families, when they are in need. It does this by making grants to individuals through their Regiments and Corps and supporting a wide range of specialist charities that sustain the British Army 'family' both at home and around the world.

Taking pride in being responsive, making a difference at a critical point in people's lives. The Soldiers' Charity has been doing this since 1944, working with veterans of every conflict, and it envisage continuing doing so for the 'long haul' – supporting all future generations of our soldiers and their dependents.

Opposite: Mark Lloyd with his thoughts at the Menin Gate

Above: The Thiepval Memorial to the Missing on the Somme.

Left: A little stroll through the woods.

Friendships are soon made among complete strangers sharing a common bond.

It was during the First World War that initial thoughts were given to the Nation's servicemen and the need to raise funds to help with their welfare both physically and mentally. As early as 1917, the Royal Navy saw the foundation of the King George's Fund for Sailors. In 1919 the Ex Service Mental Welfare Society and the Royal Air Force Benevolent Fund were formed, followed in 1921 by the Royal British Legion. There was, however, no specific charitable body linked to the Army. This was remedied when the Army Benevolent Fund [ABF] came into being with the inaugural meeting of the board on 23 August 1944. From that moment the focus of the ABF has been to support the men and women of the British Army through hardships, be they caused by operational matters or through other issues.

Funding for the charity began slowly, initially with requests to Regimental Associations and then by public donation. This funding continues today from many avenues, from private and public donation,

Above: Traversing a woodland path on day two.

Below: Ambassador Philip 'Barney' Gillespie at the Thiepval Memorial.

gift aid donations and event sponsorships both corporate and individual. In 1947, for example, the Charity produced the film 'Men At Arms' which was shown in cinemas nationwide and raised £49,557 in funds. In 1964 the Charity produced its first Christmas Cards for sale and in 1967 the first 'Soldiers Day' was held in London. Soldiers themselves have assisted in the fundraising since 1972 when the 'Day's Pay Scheme' was introduced.

In recognising the need to move forward, the Army Benevolent Fund decided to rebrand and it is now known as ABF The Soldiers' Charity. It continues to provide the support needed by so many, and the words of its vision today hold fast to the aims established in 1944:

"That all soldiers, veterans and their immediate families should have the opportunity to avoid hardship and enjoy independence and dignity."

In recognising the need to move forward, the Army Benevolent Fund decided to rebrand and it is now known as ABF The Soldiers' Charity.

Walker Alex Geddes in Flat Iron Copse Cemetery.

Always time for tea.

CHAPTER 2

THE AMBASSADORS

Colonel Andy Reid MBE: 2016

Colonel Andy Reid of the 3rd Battalion, Yorkshire Regiment had served for 13 years, when in October 2009, while on patrol in Helmand Province, Afghanistan, he was blown up by an improvised explosive device. He was injured so badly that it was thought he would not survive. Andy defied the odds to the extent that, within a month, he was able to meet up with members of his patrol again. What he has achieved since then is little short of unbelievable. Despite losing both legs and an arm, he has undertaken two tandem skydives, taken part in the St Helen's 10K Run, abseiled down the Big One in Blackpool, and countless other activities.

Andy was medically discharged from the Army and in late 2012 became a father to William; in 2018, his wife Claire gave birth to their daughter Scarlett. His autobiography *Standing Tall: The Inspirational Story of a True British Hero* was published in 2013, and is a powerful read.

Andy's attitude to life is 'I am a survivor, not a victim', and he wants to show the world he can do anything. On the last day of the walk in 2016, when most people were struggling with blisters, exhaustion and various aches and pains, Andy stood in front of the walkers at The Ploegsteert Memorial near Ypres, pointed to the nearby graves in the cemetery and said "these men are the victims – I went home but they didn't." His words were such that the walkers were all inspired to dig deep and make the final push towards the Menin Gate and the finish line. In further recognition of his charitable works in February 2019 Andy Reid was appointed to the post of Honorary Colonel to the Merseyside Army Cadet Force.

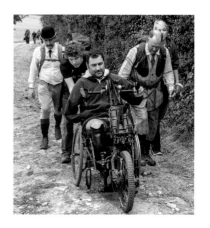

Opposite: Andy at the Vimy Memorial.

These men are the victims – I went home but they didn't.

Stewart Harris: 2017

Former Guardsman Stewart Harris served with 1st Battalion, Welsh Guards. Whilst on tour in Afghanistan in 2012, a roadside bomb hurled Stewart's vehicle into a ditch, leaving him with brain damage; the impact of this has left him partially sighted and partially deaf. The same year he also witnessed three of his comrades shot dead by an Afghan policeman. Stewart was later diagnosed with Post Traumatic Stress Disorder before leaving the Army at the age of 30, the culmination of 13 years' service.

To be where so many of my countrymen fell was an incredible experience for me.

Stewart Harris laying a wreath at the Menin Gate.

During his transition from Army to civilian life, whilst struggling to come to terms with his diagnosis, Stewart would experience further upset. In 2014 a burglary took place at Stewart's home in Rhyl, North Wales which he shared with his wife, Rhian, and their two young daughters. The thieves took off with the family's car, household items, as well as Stewart's glasses, upon which he relies heavily since sustaining his injuries on tour.

He says of the experience:

"Aside from being burgled, which is a horrible feeling... When someone enters your house without you even knowing, where your children sleep... It haunted me for a long time. I took a massive step back in my recovery."

ABF The Soldiers' Charity stepped in to help Stewart and his family during this upsetting time. The family were reliant upon the fixed income from Stewart's Army pension, but the costs quoted by various security companies were simply beyond what the family could afford. The Soldiers' Charity provided a grant towards the purchase and installation of CCTV cameras at the family home – assistance that was granted rapidly and without fuss:

"To ask for help and then to be told 'yes that's going to be fine' is absolutely amazing... The weight of the world was taken off my shoulders."

Stewart is now an Ambassador for the Charity and in 2017 he took part in The Frontline Walk.

"I really wanted to see where the 38th Welsh Division fought so bravely at Mametz Wood during the Battle of the Somme. To be where so many of my countrymen fell was an incredible experience for me."

21

Left: Bob in St Symphorian Military Cemetery, Mons.

Opposite: Bob Semple tells his story on the first night at Arras.

Bob Semple: 2017 / 2018

Bob Semple served in the Royal Engineers, and after leaving the Army gained employment in the oil industry. His work regularly took him to the Middle East and it was during one of these trips to Yemen in early 2014, that Bob was ambushed and captured by Al Qaeda. He was then held in solitary confinement for the next 18 months, with his legs chained to a wall in a windowless barely lit, cell.

During this time, his wife Sallie was supporting the couple's three sons and the family home with no idea whether she would ever see Bob alive again. In addition to the stress of not knowing if Bob would ever return or even if he was still alive, Sallie had to deal with the financial pressures of stretching her nurse's salary to cover the cost of her busy household.

Bob had been captive for over a year before Sallie began to look for help. Within days of hearing about Sallie's situation, The Soldiers' Charity stepped in to help, assisting Sallie with the costs towards her household bills. She later said,

"I was overwhelmed when the Charity stepped in to help. It was such a weight off our shoulders with so much else going on. I was just taking one day at a time, but we never knew when the phone rang if it would be the kidnappers, or Bob, or the news we were dreading."

On 22 August 2015, having been blindfolded in the boot of a car for more than ten hours, Bob was rescued. The boot burst open and he felt a hand on his arm and someone telling him, "You're safe now."

On several occasions Bob believed this time would never come. He recalls the times he believed he was close to death:

> *"They took me out into the sand on a number of occasions, each time I thought 'this is it'. Each time they made videos. They wanted me to beg and cry but I wouldn't."*

Bob was therefore delighted when he completed The Frontline Walk in 2017 and inspired others to carry on despite their aches and pains.

Phillip (Barney) Gillespie: 2018

Phillip, more commonly known as Barney, was 16 years old when he joined The Royal Irish Regiment in 2004. He deployed on his first tour of Afghanistan in 2006, and then again on a second tour in 2008. In 2010, despite being just 22 years old, he deployed as a section commander on his third tour of the country. Four months into the tour Barney stepped on an improvised explosive device whilst out on a patrol. As a result of the explosion he lost his right leg. He says:

> *"There was a ferocious sound; I was blown off the ground and landed back on the device. My foot was completely gone; I could see the bone from my shin to my knee. Straight away I knew that life as I knew it had changed; will I walk again? Will my girlfriend stay with me? How will my dad cope?"*

After being evacuated back to Camp Bastion, Barney needed three operations before being flown to the Queen Elizabeth Hospital in Birmingham. He describes seeing his missing limb for the first time:

> *"A horrifying sight. Every second, every minute, every day for two weeks I replayed the incident in my head but then decided what was the point? It's not about what happened, it's about moving forward.*

Barney and his dad in
Fauberg de Amiens
British Cemetery Arras.

*From then on it was all about rehabilitation, physio and prosthetic
legs. You realise that it wasn't your fault, you were in a war zone,
things like this happen."*

He was then transferred to the Defence Services Medical Rehabilitation
Centre at Headley Court and within two weeks was learning to walk on
a prosthetic leg. Over the next year physiotherapy was Barney's priority
but he faced spending Christmas alone in hospital when he urgently
needed another operation. His partner Kirsty couldn't afford to travel from
Ballymena to Wiltshire to be with him, so The Soldiers' Charity stepped in
with a grant to cover her travel and subsistence costs. Further funding was
provided so his home could be adapted to his disability. Barney says:

*"The Soldiers' Charity are unsung heroes, they just do the work
and get on with the job quickly and quietly without any limelight or
praise. The key thing for me is the aftercare that they provide, whether
support once home from hospital or for the older generation. You
know that they'll always be there, just ticking away quietly."*

*It's not about what
happened, it's about
moving forward ... You
realize that it wasn't
your fault, you were
in a war zone, things
like this happen.*

25

CHAPTER 3

THE SOLDIERS' CHARITY STAFF

Brigadier (Ret'd) Robin Bacon
Chief of Staff

Brigadier (Ret'd) Robin Bacon served in the Army for 32 years, first as a logistician and latterly as an HR policy strategist. He joined ABF The Soldiers' Charity in March 2010 as the Chief of Staff, and has enjoyed every aspect of being part of a great team, delivering fantastic support to those in need. He has participated on the Frontline Walk every year since the inaugural walk in 2014. Robin is a figurehead of The Frontline Walk, his imposing stature and leadership skills providing motivation to the walkers and staff.

Opposite: Robin Bacon, ABF The Soldiers' Charity Chief of Staff gives the oration at the Menin Gate.

Colonel (Ret'd) Helen McMahon MBE
Case Studies Liaison Manager

Helen has worked for the ABF The Soldiers' Charity since 2010, following a successful career in the Army. She was commissioned into the Army in 1979, serving for 32 years in the UK and Germany and undertaking operational tours in Northern Ireland, Bosnia and Kosovo. Whilst in Northern Ireland, Helen was mentioned in dispatches (MiD) and later received an MBE for her services.

Colonel (Retd') Helen McMahon at the Vimy Memorial.

Amy Kenyon
Events Manager

The Frontline Walk would never have got off the ground without the unassuming star qualities of Events Manager, Amy Kenyon. Amy joined the charity in 2014 and was given the task of setting up and managing The Frontline Walk. Within weeks Amy had recruited a team of 30 people who completed the inaugural walk. Amy's charisma, cheerfulness and quiet determination are some of the values that explain why the Walk has gone from strength to strength. She is responsible for working with Classic Challenge and ensuring the walkers are looked after, whilst at the same time raising over £1.25m since 2014. Without Amy, there would be no Frontline Walk. Amy has herself completed the challenge every year, even doing both walks in 2018. She is an expert at dealing with daft questions!

Steve Oatley
Head of National Events

Amy works closely with Steve Oatley, Head of National Events at the Charity. Steve manages a team of seven people and has been with the charity for ten years. He is responsible for managing 25 events each year, and is also a mainstay of The Frontline Walk. Steve wanders along, quietly encouraging others, and never seems to be suffering any aches and pains.

Amy (centre), Henri (second from right) and Steve (far right) lead the way.

Above: Robin and Andy at Wellington Barracks.

Below: Ed in action.

Henri Stewart
Executive Assistant to the Chief Executive and Chief of Staff

Henri, an Army Reservist, joined the charity as Executive Assistant to the Chief Executive and Chief of Staff in 2013, following her return from an operational tour in Afghanistan. She has participated in The Frontline Walk since its inception in 2014, both as a staff member and as a fundraiser, and is enormously proud to be part of such a great team.

Ed Smith

Ed Smith is responsible for the 'action' photographs in this book. A professional photographer since 2006, Ed is at home in the wide open spaces of France and Belgium. He was formerly ranked amongst the world's leading white-water kayakers and is proficient across the spectrum of adventure sports. Walkers are often amazed as they see Ed running past them to capture an unusual or interesting shot. He never seems to tire and covers as many miles as the walkers themselves. He is a real team man and is often the last man out of the Old Bill Pub in Ypres on the final nights of the Western Front walk.

CHAPTER 4

THE WALK HISTORIANS

Steve Roberts: 2016 / 2017 / 2018

It was whilst guiding a battlefield tour in October 2014 that Steve first came across The Frontline Walk, both in the hotel the two groups were sharing and when he bumped into groups of walkers along the route.

As an old soldier (a Red Cap), Steve had always been a supporter of service charities and when the opportunity to act as the historian for the walk came along in 2016 he jumped at the chance. Both of Steve's grandfathers served on the Western Front and it was through them that his passion for the actions and stories of the First World War developed.

Left: Steve gives the initial brief at Arras.

Opposite: Walker Ian Houghton paying his respects in Rifle House Cemetery.

Steve's grandfather Private William Roberts, East Yorkshire Regiment.

For Steve, as a professional military historian and battlefield guide, The Frontline Walk enables him to share his passion whilst helping the charity at the same time.

"Being able to tell the stories of the men who went before us is vitally important, and if I can do that whilst making the route come alive for the walkers then I have done a good job. Not just for the The Soldiers' Charity or the walkers, but for those who went before us, those who served, those who died and those who came home and got on with their lives. Men like my grandfathers, Private Henry Goddard of the Middlesex Regiment and Private William Roberts of the East Yorkshire Regiment and the Royal Engineers."

Below: Steve describing events on the first day of the Somme.

Terry Whenham: 2014 / 2016 / 2017 / 2018

"You had a great-uncle who died on the Somme." These words were said to Terry by his dad, who had served in the Royal Army Service Corps during the Second World War, when he was a young boy. Those words stuck with him throughout his childhood and into his teens. Then, one day, in April 2001, a search on the Commonwealth War Graves Commission website found Henry Stephen Whenham, 6th Battalion of the East Kent (The Buffs) Regiment who had died of wounds on 4 August 1916 and was buried in a cemetery in Northern France. Two weeks later he found himself at Henry's graveside and wondering what had happened to him, the younger brother of his grandfather, Arthur. It was a life-changing moment for Terry. Over the next few years he pieced together Henry's short life and his army career, and discovered that his death had changed his family history. His dad told him how his father, Arthur, had served throughout the First World War in the Royal Garrison Artillery.

Terry was very proud to discover that Arthur had been awarded the Distinguished Conduct Medal for gallantry in 1915. Henry was a volunteer who had joined the Army at the outbreak of war in August 1914. He had left behind a girlfriend called Dolly, who he had intended to marry after the war. Tragedy struck the Whenham family, and Dolly, on Thursday 3 August 1916

Above: Terry's great-uncle Henry Whenham.

Right: 'Tommy' – Terry's First World War bear.

when Henry was wounded in a night attack against a German position called 'Ration Trench'. This was during the infamous Battle of the Somme. Henry was evacuated from the trenches and taken to an Advanced Dressing Station close by. Incredibly, his brother Arthur saw him lying on a stretcher. Henry was then transferred to a Field Ambulance Station at Bouzincourt, where he died the following day and where he is now buried. After the war, Arthur was demobbed from the Army. He had consoled Dolly about the death of her loved one. They fell in love and married in 1919. They became Terry's grandparents. On that cold April day Terry stared at the family epitaph on Henry's headstone. It read:

"He died so that we may live."

Then it occurred to him. If Henry had lived he would have married Dolly and his dad and Terry would not have been born. A cold shiver went down his spine that day. In 2014 Terry was one of the first to sign up for The Frontline Walk. In 2016, he walked alongside Jenny Baulk whose relative had served in the same Battalion as Henry. They paused at the very spot where Henry was mortally wounded and thought of their relatives. Jenny's relative was killed a few weeks later and is featured in this book. Terry would like to dedicate this book to his great-uncle Henry and grandfather Arthur.

If Henry had lived he would have married Dolly and my dad and I would not have been born. A cold shiver went down my spine that day.

34

Vern Littley: 2018

Vern Littley, served in the Royal Artillery for 26 years leaving in 2011 with the rank of Warrant Officer Class 2. Whilst deployed in Iraq in 2005, he was in a vehicle that was blown up by a roadside bomb. It wasn't until three years after he had left the Army that he was diagnosed with Post Traumatic Stress Disorder, and he has battled with the effects of what is termed 'survivor's guilt' ever since. The Soldiers' Charity recruited Vern as one of the historians for the 2018 Last Hundred Days Offensive Walk. It proved to be a turning point in Vern's fight with his PTSD. Vern explained how being part of The Frontline Walk has helped him:

Vern's great-uncle
Harry Thomas Wells.

"My great-uncle, Harry Thomas Wells of 7th Battalion, Royal West Kent Regiment, was killed at the battle of Le Cateau, 23 October 1918. He was my great-grandmother's brother and she was heavily involved in his upbringing as a boy. When the news of his death was received a single tear ran down my great-grandfather's face at the dining room table. A few years ago, another of Harry's relatives, Carol Ravenhill, discovered a letter that his Commanding Officer sent to the family explaining how he was killed. I have been aware of Harry since childhood; my dad and I marked the 100th anniversary of his death with a trip to Mons. As the sun went down on the second day of the walk, we passed the cemetery where Harry is buried and it was a truly amazing experience for me. As an artilleryman, Le Cateau is hallowed ground and it was wonderful for me to talk to The Frontline Walkers about the three members of the Royal Field Artillery, who earned the Victoria Cross there on 26 August 1914. It was a dream come true for me.

Being part of The Frontline Walk extended family gave me the chance to come to terms with my PTSD and survivor's guilt. I was part of something very special and was completely different to the other tours I have guided. It was not just about being an historian but supporting the walkers when they needed help, if only throwing a bag of sweets at them!"

At the lunch stop on day two, Vern captivated the walkers and support teams with a heartfelt tribute to Harry, whilst holding a photograph of him. One of the many moments on the 2018 walk that anyone who was there will never, ever forget.

CHAPTER 5

CLASSIC CHALLENGE STAFF

Classic Challenge has been leading the way in charity challenges since 1992 and have been working with our charity since 2016. Their team is responsible for all of the logistics that have been essential to the success of The Frontline Walk. Without their work, walkers would have nowhere to eat, sleep, recharge their batteries or celebrate at the final night Gala Dinner. They look after the walkers' safety and deal with any medical problems that occur frequently, such as terrible blisters, twisted joints or just total exhaustion and, in some cases, old age! These guys deserve a special mention. Several of them served in the Armed Forces so the charity is close to their heart:

Abi Davies, Support / Walker
Beth Moos, Doctor
Claude Fallik, Route planner / support
Craig Evans, Support / Medic / Walker
Emma Kramer, Support / Walker
Gavin Kramer, Support / Walker
Gideon Seligman, Walk Manager
Jo Richardson, Paramedic support
Julian Bromley, Doctor
Lee McKay, Paramedic support
Lucy Thomas, GOC logistics
Matt Ladbrook, Doctor
Stuart Bigg, Lead walker

Above: The Classic Challenge team at Vimy Ridge Memorial.

Opposite: Lucy, the Classic GOC Logistics at Tyne Cot.

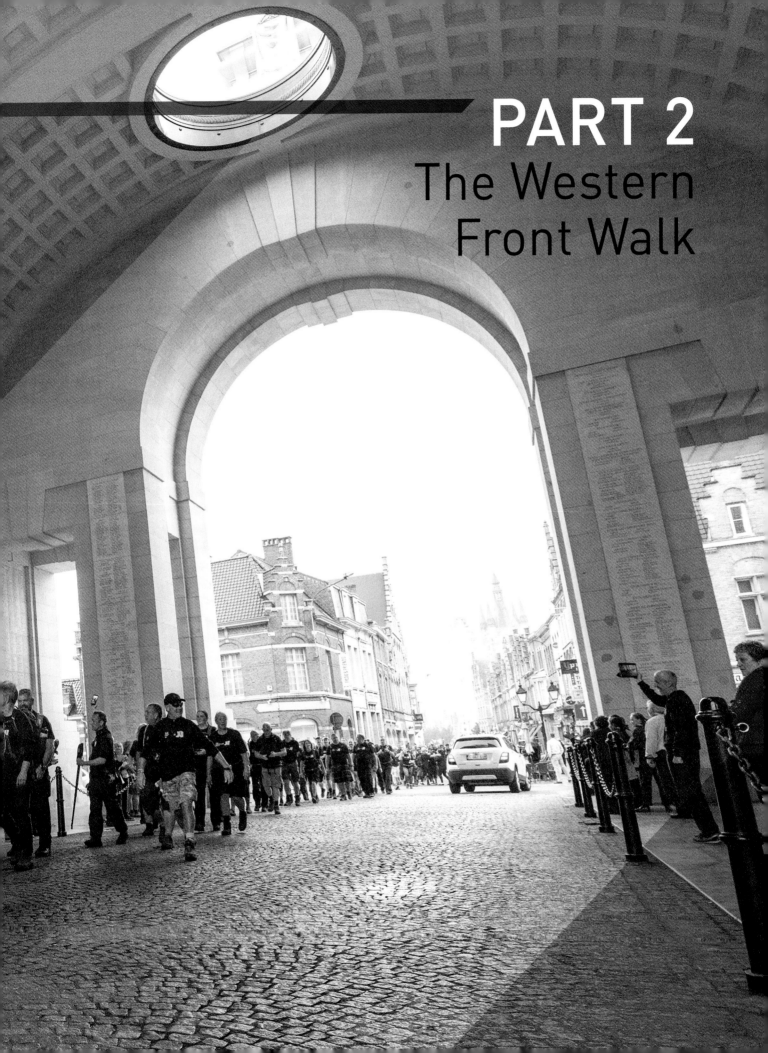

PART 2
The Western Front Walk

CHAPTER 6

DAY 1: THE SOMME

Historically, The Frontline Walk has taken the walkers over three different battlefields of the Western Front. Each day walkers crossed what are now peaceful landscapes, but were once battlefields, enshrined in history. At various points along the route they were given historical briefs about the route and the stories of the individuals in whose steps they were walking. Many of those walking had their own stories and thoughts to follow and it was important to put the route into context for them.

Moving over the 1916 Battlefields of the Somme, the first day's walking focused mainly on ground fought over on 1 July 1916, the opening day of the Battle of the Somme, but also moved through areas of later fighting. During the course of the day the walkers passed many of the Commonwealth War Graves Commission Cemeteries which cover the landscape. There are far too many to include here but suffice to say individuals diverted from the route to visit as many as they could.

The Somme

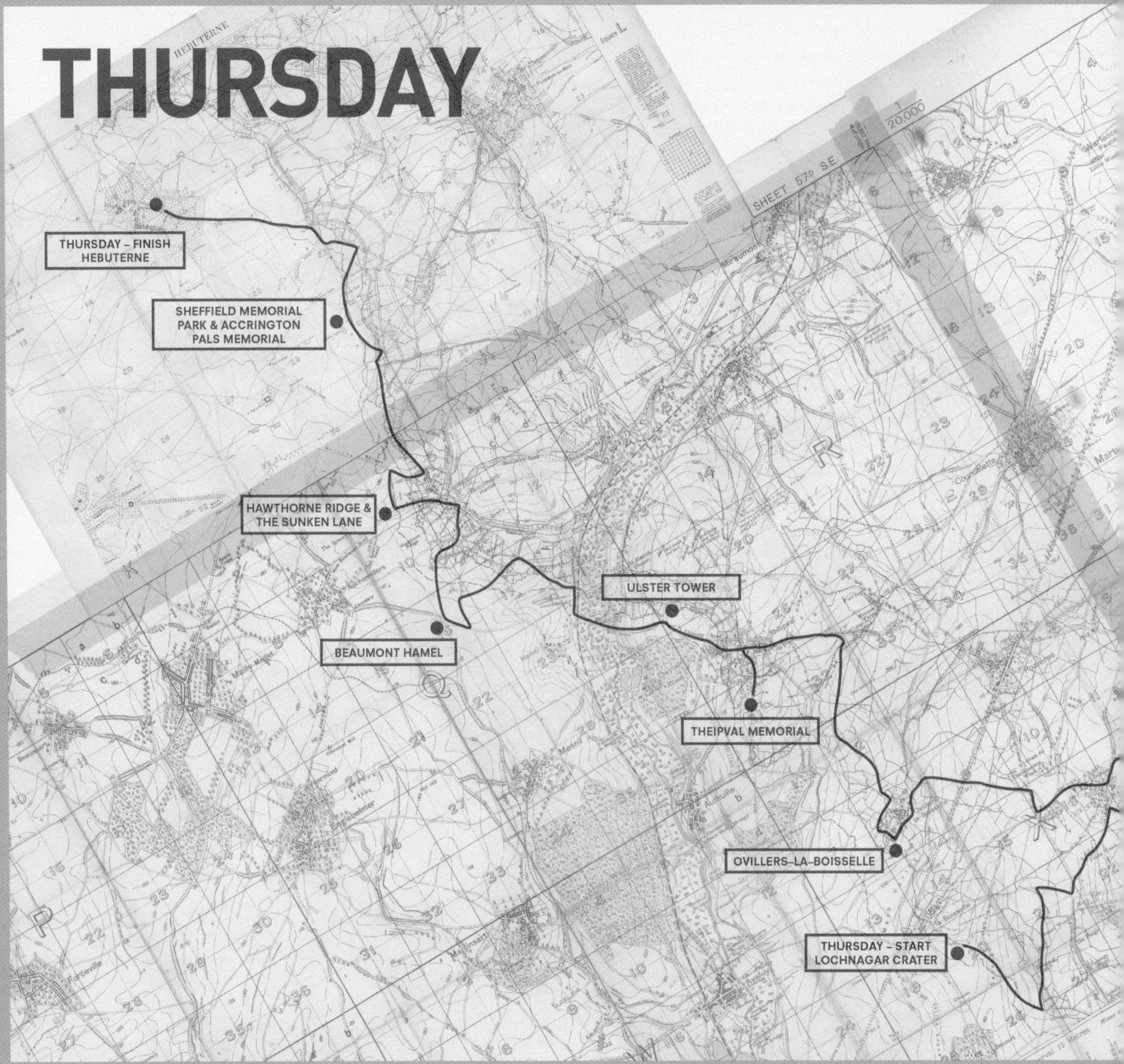

THURSDAY

THURSDAY – FINISH
HEBUTERNE

SHEFFIELD MEMORIAL
PARK & ACCRINGTON
PALS MEMORIAL

HAWTHORNE RIDGE &
THE SUNKEN LANE

ULSTER TOWER

BEAUMONT HAMEL

THEIPVAL MEMORIAL

OVILLERS–LA–BOISSELLE

THURSDAY – START
LOCHNAGAR CRATER

Day 1: Thursday

Start: Lochnagar Crater, the location of the start of the Battle of the Somme.

Finish: Hébuterne Military Cemetery.

Distance: 34km

Highlights:

- 38th Welsh Division Memorial

- Flatiron Copse Cemetery

- Thiepval Memorial to the Missing

- Sunken Lane

The German attack on the town and fortifications of Verdun in January 1916 had brought about the Anglo/French attack on the Somme. It was intended to divert German resources away from Verdun and to give the French the opportunity to replenish and to commit additional forces into the defence of the city. The attack commenced at 7.30am on 1 July 1916 and to mark this, the first day started at first light, when the walkers set off from the 'Lochnagar' Crater, the site of the largest underground mine exploded on the Somme. The route moved past some of the most iconic sites, and for many walkers, sites of particular relevance to them and their families. During the

Field kitchens and dug-
outs in 'Sausage Valley',
Somme.

morning the route moved from La Boiselle, through Fricourt and along
'Death Valley', passing the largest wood on the Somme, 'Mametz Wood'.
During three days in mid July 1916, the 38th (Welsh) Division suffered over
4,000 casualties attacking the wood, and it is there that walkers visit the
Division's 'Dragon' Memorial.

   The morning break was taken at 'Flat Iron Copse' Cemetery, and the
route then continued towards Contalmaison, through Ovillers and on to
lunch at Thiepval. Walkers always took time out from lunch to visit the
Thiepval Memorial to the Missing, to pay their respects to just under
73,000 men who have no identified graves and whose names are recorded
on the panels of the memorial.

   The second half of the day's route led the walkers past the 'Ulster Tower'
Memorial to the 36th (Ulster) Division who attacked the area and suffered
the loss of 5,000 casualties on 1 July 1916. For walker Tom Saunders it is
there that he literally walked in the footsteps of his grandfather. Climbing
the slopes away from the River Ancre, the route moved towards and

Far left: Walking wounded medical aid post.

Left: Colin Beesley, a Royal Artillery veteran.

Below left: A welcome beer at the end of the day.

In the trenches at Thiepval.

through the 'Newfoundland Memorial Park' where walkers have always been given a warm welcome by the Canadian students who staff the memorial. Passing through the trenches, the walkers continued towards Beaumont Hamel, and the Hawthorn Mine Crater, before moving down the slope to the afternoon break near the 'Sunken Lane'.

Prior to leaving the afternoon break stop, walkers were told the story of the men of the Lancashire Fusiliers on 1 July 1916 and listened to the voice of one who was there, played over a loudspeaker. The route then passed over the 'Redan Ridge' towards the 'Sheffield Memorial Park' and the ground over which the 31st Division advanced to their deaths on 1 July 1916. On leaving the area opposite Serre, the route continued towards the finish line in the village of Hebuterne where the sight of the local bar and a cold beer were always welcomed by all.

Jenny Baulk: 2016

Private's Albert Gore and Henry Whenham had much in common. Both had volunteered for the army in 1914 and joined the 6th Battalion, East Kent Regiment (The Buffs). They trained and served together. Both men saw action at the Hohenzollern Redoubt near Loos in March 1916 and in the early stages of the Battle of the Somme.

On 3 August 1916, Henry Whenham was one of 118 casualties suffered by the Battalion during an attack on a German strongpoint near Ovillers. He died of his wounds the following day. A few weeks later, Albert Gore was also killed, along with 128 other men during an attack near Gueudecourt. Both men were aged 20 when they died.

Almost 100 years later, Albert and Henry's descendants, Jenny Baulk and Terry Whenham, found themselves walking together on The Frontline Walk.

Like her friend Laura Bowkett, Jenny found the walk incredibly challenging but rewarding:

"We started the trek at the incredible Lochnager Crater and it seemed the most fitting place to start. Over the next couple of days, despite our preparation, I don't think any amount of training would have prepared both Laura and I for the pain we would both feel. Laura suffered from terrible blisters and I had knee problems and it felt like it was going to give up on me at any moment.

Without Laura and the other walkers I would not have finished the challenge. We experienced every emotion and I cannot thank everyone enough for the support they gave me during the trek. Sadly the last six miles of day two, Laura was told by the medics that she needed to rest, which she didn't accept without a fight. I felt like I had lost my right arm. As I approached the top of Vimy Ridge, the pain

The Medal Index Card of Private Albert Gore.

Jenny in the centre,
with Terry on the left
and Laura right.

seemed to ease when I saw Laura in the distance, in the shadow of the
towering memorial to missing Canadian soldiers.

Day three was not just physically but mentally challenging too. Not once
did we consider giving up, despite the pain. The end was in sight and
we trudged on. On the outskirts of Ypres we re-grouped as a team and
started the slow walk up towards the memorial. Even now it brings my
hair up on ends and the overwhelming feeling of emotion that brought
Laura and I to tears. The pain we had experienced soon vanished with
the pride bursting through as we realised we had followed in the footsteps
of such young, brave and courageous men that we owed everything to.

From visiting the many graves, learning about horrific stories these
men and some children went through to being able to pay my respects
to Albert at Thiepval. Doing this along with Andy Reid, a serving
soldier injured in Afghanistan, my good friend Laura, Terry and the
rest of the team, made this one of the most truly humbling experiences
that I will never forget.

We Will Remember Them."

As I approached the top of Vimy Ridge, the pain seemed to ease when I saw Laura in the distance, in the shadow of the towering memorial to missing Canadian soldiers.

Steve Bish: 2017

Steve signed up for The Frontline Walk one Sunday afternoon in April 2017 and within a couple of weeks his brother Andrew had decided to join him. *"We decided to dedicate our participation to the memory of our grandfather who had survived the First World War but died before we were born."*

William Bish was born in Nottingham in November 1886, he joined the army five months before his 18th birthday, enlisting in the Sherwood Foresters. When war broke out in 1914, William, who was by then married and had three children was immediately recalled from the reserves for service. He re-trained as a medic and went to France with 19th Field Ambulance, Royal Army Medical Corps in November 1914.

For the next four months the unit was based in Armentières and it was in February 1915 that another daughter was born and christened Ada Armentieres Gordon Bish. Armentières was clearly a connection with William, but opinion is divided in the family as to whether the name Gordon was in tribute to General 'Gordon of Khartoum' or whether it was another officer that William was serving under in France.

William survived the war and ended up becoming the proud father of 13 children. In 1920 he joined 5th (Hunts) Battalion Northamptonshire Regiment of the Territorial Army and was promoted to Warrant Officer the following year. He passed away in December 1955 after suffering from Bronchitis.

"On the first morning of the walk we passed through Mametz Wood; for Andy and I we were quite literally walking in our grandfather's footsteps. It was quite a moment! It was not long after the emotion of Mametz Wood that it began to rain, and after about an hour or so of fairly heavy showers we were subjected to an almighty cloudburst which saw us all absolutely drenched regardless of our waterproofs. It was later that day when the weather had changed completely and it seemed like a late summer sunny afternoon when the second 'emotional moment' hit home. We'd all dried off and were enjoying the sunshine when it dawned on us that no matter in which direction we looked, we could see cemeteries and memorials of differing sizes.

Those of us walking for the first time were prepared for the physical challenges of the walk, but the emotional side was a bit of a shock to many and it could creep up at any time.

Those of us walking for the first time were prepared for the physical challenges of the walk but the emotional side was a bit of a shock to many and it could creep up at any time.

I'm extremely glad to have taken part and have made countless new friends in doing so. My initial concern about raising the required amount of sponsorship for such an important charity proved groundless as Andrew and myself more than doubled our initial target by collecting over £5,000 between us! Just writing these words have brought back so many fantastic memories that my next task will undoubtedly be to signing up for The Frontline Walk again."

Nicole Goodwin: 2016

"So many men died in combat or of their wounds. Being a soldier in any war is a dangerous occupation. We remember those soldiers that are killed in action or succumb to their wounds. But also recorded amongst the casualty figures are men who died of illness, disease and as a result of accidents."

Sisters Nicole Goodwin, a marketing director from Birmingham, and Louise Robiati, a serving Army doctor, completed The Frontline Walk in memory of their great-uncle, Alexander Black. Serving with 9th Battalion, Black Watch, Alexander was one of those men who did not die in action but was instead the victim of an accident. The entry relating to Alexander in the 'Register of Soldiers' Effects' records his cause of death simply as 'accident'.

By August 1916 the Battle of the Somme was in full swing and the 9th Battalion, Black Watch had already suffered a number of casualties including 137 casualties on 18 August 1916 alone. During their few days in the frontline near Contalmaison they had suffered 249 casualties.

On 4 September 1916, 9th Battalion, Black Watch moved into Shelter Wood preparing to support an attack on High Wood.

At some point the following day, 5 September 1916, Alexander was involved in some form of accident. There is no record of any incident in the battalion War diary and no casualties are recorded that day; as such we can only guess at what happened. Whatever the cause, by the end of 5 September 1916, Alexander had been killed, aged 22.

He was taken the short distance from Shelter Wood to a small copse nearby known as Peake Wood. Adjacent to the copse was a newly established cemetery, and it was there that Alexander was laid to rest.

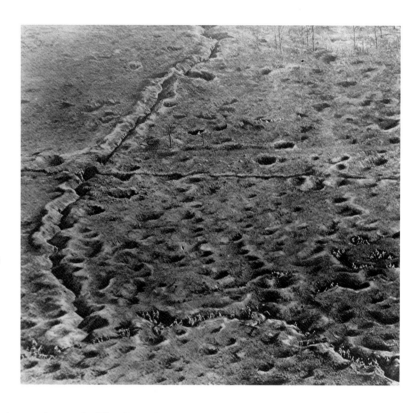

Sadly, at some later stage, his grave was lost in subsequent fighting and he is now commemorated with a memorial headstone in the cemetery.

Today the cemetery contains just 103 burials and commemorations of the First World War. It also contains special memorials to six casualties believed to be buried there but whose graves could not be located, including Alexander.

Shelter Wood, where the accident happened, had been captured by the British on 3 July 1916. According to some accounts it was found to be *"full of German corpses."*

Just over 100 years later Nicole and Louise took part in The Frontline Walk and, within an hour of the start, they found themselves walking near Shelter Wood.

Birdseye view of a battlefield on the Somme front.

Simon Last: 2014 / 2016 / 2018

Simon Last from Southend on Sea, is the owner of Charnwood Genealogy and has completed The Frontline Walk on three occassions. Simon was aware of a distant relation, Peter Last, who had been wounded in the first few weeks of the war. He had been evacuated to England but had died of his injuries and was buried in Woodbridge Cemetery. Sadly, his wife Annie died ten years later aged just 39.

In 2012 Simon researched all 75 men with the surname Last who had been killed during the First World War. The first one he found was Leonard

Above: William Last buried at Delville Wood on the Somme.

Right: William Last's will, written shortly before he was killed.

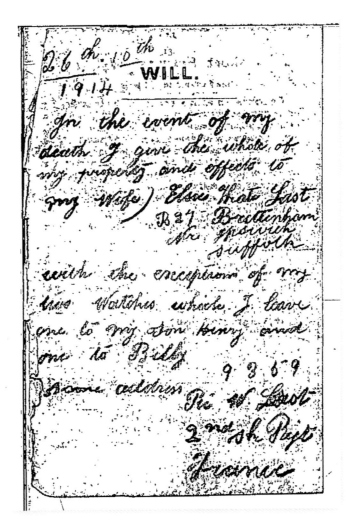

Walkers pause at the 38th (Welsh)
Division Memorial at Mametz Wood.

Last who had died just two days before Christmas 1916. Leonard, originally from Suffolk, had emigrated to Australia prior to the war and in 1914 had joined the Australian Imperial Force. Back in England, Leonard's mother and sister had to deal with the dreadful loss of Leonard. To make it worse Leonard's father had committed suicide the year before, aged 55. Leonard is buried in Delville Wood cemetery, not far from where he fell.

Simon then discovered a will made by his namesake, William Simon Last who had died on 2 March 1916. It read:

> *"In the event of my death I give the whole of my effects to my wife Elsie Kate with the exception of my two watches, which I leave to my son Henry and one to Billy – Pte W Last 9359 2nd Suffolk Regiment, France."*

Although no relation, these soldiers' stories inspired Simon to complete The Frontline Walk three times, raising over £10,000 for the charity. Simon explained how these soldiers' stories affected him:

> *"I find these personal stories really resonate with me when I am taking part in The Frontline Walk and walking in the footsteps of these young men from over 100 years ago. There is something about being in the places and locations in France and Belgium that before were just words, names in documents and books and it doesn't matter how many times I visit I still get those feelings."*

Chris Mullane: 2017

Chris completed the 2017 walk with his wife Maria. He always knew that his great-uncle Daniel had been killed whilst serving with the 1st Battalion, Welsh Guards in September 1916 during the Battle of the Somme, but didn't know where or how it had happened. Family legend spoke of Daniel being killed as he was helping a wounded officer.

Daniel has no known grave and his name is recorded on the Thiepval Memorial to the Missing. Over 72,000 men are commemorated on the memorial. Built on one of the highest points of the battlefield, it can be seen from miles around. It truly reflects the terrible tragedy of the 'Great Push' as it was known to the soldiers.

It was pouring with rain and blowing a gale as Chris and Maria approached Pier 7D. Chris stood back and stood in silence for a few seconds before saying two simple words, *"Oh wow!"*

One of the charity's researchers' had previously researched an officer of the same Battalion, 2nd Lieutenant Alexander Piggott Wernher who had fought in the same action. On 10 September 1916, the Welsh Guards took part in an attack on German positions east of Ginchy. The night was very dark, and on arriving at Ginchy much rifle-fire was encountered. In the ruins of the village they came across small parties of Germans, who all immediately surrendered.

The following morning there was very little light and a thin mist hovering over the area. As the men prepared to continue

I find these personal stories really resonate with me when I am taking part in The Frontline Walk and walking in the footsteps of these young men from over 100 years ago.

All hell broke loose as machine guns opened up on us from the front and from the flank. We stood no chance and the boys were everywhere falling, but we kept moving forward.

– Private Albert Evans, 16th (Cardiff City) Battalion, Welsh Regiment

the assault, the Germans suddenly launched a strong counter-attack in an attempt to regain Ginchy and Delville Wood.

Although Wernher was himself shot in the leg, his company managed to keep the Germans at bay. As he was being carried out of the danger zone, he was hit again and killed. Chris' family had told him that Daniel had been killed carrying an officer, perhaps it was Alexander? Two different stories could have possibly merged into one!

Daniel's older brother Peter, served as a Corporal in the Welsh Regiment. He had survived the war but on 7 July 1916, Peter, took part in the 38th (Welsh) Division's first attempt to capture Mametz Wood. Attacking towards the 'Hammerhead' his Battalion was decimated by machine gun fire coming from inside the wood and from Flatiron Copse on their right.

They suffered 283 casualties and the attack failed. Private Albert Evans, 16th (Cardiff City) Battalion, Welsh Regiment wrote:

> *"All hell broke loose as machine guns opened up on us from the front and from the flank. We stood no chance and the boys were everywhere falling, but we kept moving forward."*

The 38th Division attacked the wood again three days later and despite heavy fighting, captured the wood. On the first day of The Frontline Walk, Chris walked in what was 'No Man's Land' on that terrible day. He didn't realise at the time that his relative had served there. When he found out he said *"I feel very emotional and very proud. I am a bit lost for words at the moment."*

Troops advance during the Battle of Ginchy, 9 September 1916.

Paul Sansom: 2017 / 2018

Discovering that Paul had signed up for The Frontline Walk and had no family member to commemorate, his friend Kate Goddard asked Paul to remember her great-grandfather, Lance Corporal Horace Alexander of 1/7th Battalion, Middlesex Regiment.

During the Battle of Flers/Courcelette on 15 September 1916, Horace's Battalion was ordered to attack German positions within Leuze Wood and Bouleaux Wood. The attack started at 8.20am but despite support from tanks, being used for the first time on the Western Front, it was quickly repulsed. The Battalion suffered the loss of some 300 casualties, of which 125 men were killed.

The following day the 1/7th Middlesex were withdrawn for a few days rest behind the lines. The rest did not last long and on 21 September 1916 the battalion returned to the frontline in the area of Leuze Wood. They remained in the line until the night of 24–25 September 1916 when they moved back into reserve trenches.

The Battalion War Diary fails to record any casualties that day, but the Commonwealth War Graves Commission records detail two men from the Battalion who died that day. Although it is now impossible to be certain, it is likely that Horace was killed by shellfire during the withdrawal that night somewhere near Leuze Wood. He is now recorded with 125 of his comrades on the Thiepval Memorial to the Missing of the Somme.

Horace's service record revealed another tragedy. Shortly after Horace had joined the army his wife Ethel had also died, so his daughter Maud was now an orphan.

On the first day of The Frontline Walk in 2017, Paul found Horace's name on the Thiepval Memorial to the Missing and placed a cross in memory of his friend's great-grandfather Horace.

Paul explained his feelings:

"I am a regular visitor to Thiepval now and every time I go there I lay a cross in memory of Horace. It gives a link to a friends' relative and brings home to me the suffering our soldiers experienced, especially as Horace is still missing. It was wonderful to be able to walk with someone in mind who paid the ultimate price."

Opposite: Thiepval Memorial to the Missing.

Horace's great-granddaughter Kate Goddard said:

Paul's great-grandfather, Ben Southwell, who served with the Army Veterinary Corps.

"It means the world to me that people such as Paul think about my great-grandad as it ensures that his memory lives on and makes his life seem less wasted somehow. It doesn't bring him back but it reminds us of the futility of war. I think it is great to support survivors of conflicts too as they have valiantly put their lives on the line so that others like us enjoy our freedom."

Paul also walked in memory of his own great-grandfather, Ben Southwell, who served with the Army Veterinary Corps throughout the war, returning home at the end to bring up his family.

Paul looking after his feet.

Tom Saunders: 2015 / 2016 / 2018

The Somme battlefield is a very special place for Tom, and for several weeks during the summer months, he gives his time to act as one of the custodians at the Ulster Memorial Tower on the Somme. Coming from Belfast, Tom is very proud of the 36th (Ulster) Division and the men who fought within it. As a custodian he regularly tells the story of the Division's battle on 1 July 1916, a story of extreme heroism. The initial successes which saw the German frontlines captured, the dogged determination needed to hold the ground, and the eventual withdrawal forced upon the men by the failure of attacks on their flanks. The Ulster Tower, built in 1921, commemorates the Division's actions on that day and the 5,000 casualties it suffered. The Tower, standing at 70 feet in height, is a lasting tribute to the men of Ulster who gave their lives during the First World War. It stands on what was the German frontline on 1 July 1916.

The Ulster Memorial Tower was erected on the site of the Schwaben Redoubt, opposite Thiepval Wood.

Tom's family connections also link him to the area and Thiepval Wood which is a short distance from the Tower. Although Tom didn't know his grandfather, Thomas Saunders, he did know that he had joined the Seaforth Highlanders in May 1915. He also discovered that he had been among the first British soldiers to arrive on the Somme battlefield in the Autumn of 1915, taking over from the French.

Despite the area having a reputation of 'live and let live', there were still casualties. In late November 1915, Thomas's Battalion suffered 29 casualties during a very heavy German artillery bombardment fired on the British trenches at Authuille, close to where the Thipeval Memorial to the

Missing now stands. Thomas became one of the casualties that day, when he was wounded in the hand by a shell fragment. Part of his finger was later amputated and he was eventually discharged from the Army.

Tom is very proud of his grandfather and always thinks about him during The Frontline Walk:

"The only family member still alive who knew my grandfather is my mother. She said he was a big, quiet and inoffensive man. She described him as an absolute gentleman. He never spoke of his experiences in the war to my dad and we only wonder what stories he must have had to tell. He was a hard-working man who returned to work in the Belfast Shipyard after the war. He was a Sergeant in the Home Guard during the second war.

Whilst I'm in the La Boisselle and Authuille areas I feel as close to him as I've ever been. I imagine him and his pals going through the daily rigours of war in preparation for the looming offensive on 1st July. His injury ensured he was home by then and I am sure he thought of his pals left behind. Having his name plaque at the Lochnagar Crater gives me a sense of his presence. I feel quite emotional when I am there."

Tom plays the flute at the start of the first days walk at Lochnagar.

A German trench at
Delville Wood, 1916.

Tim Seeley: 2014

Former soldier Tim Seeley completed The Frontline Walk in 2014, whilst
proudly carrying the Union Jack flag along the route. As he walked he
was thinking about his great-grandfather, Sergeant James Seeley MM, 8th
Battalion, Norfolk Regiment. He had been wounded in 'Delville Wood' on 19
July 1916, during the Battle of the Somme.

James had also fought with his Battalion on 1 July 1916 when they took
part in the opening day of the battle. Tim knows what happened to his
great-grandfather on that first day of the battle, because at the age of 90
James gave an interview which was published in a local paper. According to
the article James recalled:

*"On July 1st there was nothing to laugh about. There was a good deal
to cry and curse over. And for many the praying went on all day."*

James went over the top in the second wave:

*"It was our first big attack. And I remember that at about 7am they
gave us a tot of rum each. I think I had two or three because some
chaps wouldn't drink it. We were told that the German wire would
all be blown away by our artillery and it would be a walkover. Our
captain kept kidding us along. He shook my hand before we went over
and said good luck."*

Into action they went and up the hill towards Montauban. James continued:

> *"We got hung up in a shell hole – a corporal and four of us. The corporal was a quiet sort of boy, and he lifted up his head to see if anyone was about and "ping" he got a bullet through the head."*

They reached their objective and James was sent back across 'No Man's Land' to pick up rations. This is what he saw:

> *"There were blokes lying dead all over the place. British and German. It wasn't a pretty picture."*

Three weeks later James was involved in the bitter fighting in Delville Wood:

> *"The bullet struck me in the left shoulder, so I was very lucky. Another six inches to the right and it would have hit me in the head."*

James had received a much coveted 'Blighty' wound and was evacuated to hospital in England. Two years later, he found himself back on the Somme trying, alongside his mates, to stem the massive German advance of late March 1918. During the final offensive in 1918, James was awarded the Military Medal. But the interview reveals his lost mates were never far from his mind:

> *"Many of them were buried in France. We lost a lot of good men on the Somme."*

Tim remembers James fondly:

> *"The walk was very poignant for me, being a veteran, and I understand what James might have gone through and how he felt when he was shot in Delville Wood. I could only imagine the horror of the battlefields as nature has reclaimed the land but left battle scares and we have left war graves. I am extremely proud of my great-grandad and will always remember him."*

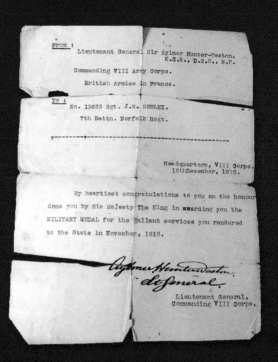

Document congratulating Tim's great-grandfather on the award of the Military Medal to him for gallantry.

Many of them were buried in France. We lost a lot of good men on the Somme.

Helen Seims: 2014 / 2016 / 2018

Helen always struggled with the physical demands of the 100km walk, but the memory of her relative Private Bertram Wadlow, 1/23rd Battalion, London Regiment, who was killed in High Wood on 15 September 1916, aged just 18, drove her on year after year.

When Bertram joined up, like so many others, he lied about his age. He was just 17 years old.

'High Wood' was a dreadful place in the summer of 1916. The British Army launched attack after attack but it took several weeks to remove the Germans from the wood. It was bitterly contested and, living up to its name, the wood dominating the surrounding battlefield, was known to the men who served there as *"The hell they called High Wood – ghastly by day, ghostly by night – the rottenest place on the Somme"*.

On that day Bertram's Battalion were in reserve and although they did not take part in the attack they still suffered casualties. Before the attack had even started, German artillery had heavily bombarded the British assembly and support trenches and subjected them to heavy rifle and machine gun fire. Caught by the German fire, the Battalion had suffered casualties even before zero hour, which had been set for 0550hrs.

The Casualty form of Bertram Wadlow recording his death.

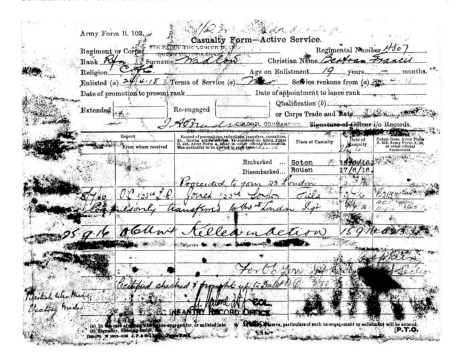

The conditions in 'High Wood' itself were almost beyond comprehension:

"The battlefield had to be imagined, for there is nothing like it on earth; in desolation, in horror, in pitifulness, in grimness. Every tree was beheaded or maimed and at the door of the wood lay a lopsided tank in a shell-hole with its nose against the base of a tree. One walked through the roots and pits and ditches that had supplanted the undergrowth, but there were worse things in the wood than sights."

The 47th Division in which Bertram served had cleared 'High Wood' of Germans after a two month stalemate. They had therefore achieved their objectives despite heavy losses. However, Haig was not impressed and commented:

"The 47th Division failed at High Wood on 15th September and the GOC was sent home! I told the Commanding Officer to teach the Division discipline and digging."

Helen walking in the footsteps of her relative, Bertram Wadlow, killed on the Somme in 1916.

Soldier poet Philip Johnstone visited the wood and, worrying about battlefield tourism after the war, wrote the following poem:

High Wood

Ladies and gentlemen, this is High Wood,
Called by the French, Bois des Fourneaux,
The famous spot which in Nineteen-Sixteen,
July, August and September was the scene
Of long and bitterly contested strife,
By reason of its High commanding site.
Observe the effect of shell-fire in the trees
Standing and fallen; here is wire; this trench
For months inhabited, twelve times changes hands;
(They soon fall in), used later as a grave.
It has been said on good authority
That in the fighting for this patch of wood
Were killed somewhere above eight thousand men,
Of whom the greater part were buried here,
This mound on which you stand being ...
Madame, please,

You are requested kindly not to touch
Or take away the Company's property
As souvenirs; you'll find we have on sale
A large variety, all guaranteed.
As I was saying, all is as it was,
This is an unknown British officer,
The tunic having lately rotten off.
Please follow me – this way ...
The path, sir, please,

The ground which was secured at great expense
The Company keeps absolutely untouched,
And in that dug-out (genuine) we provide
Refreshments at a reasonable rate.
You are requested not to leave about
Paper, or ginger-beer bottles, or orange-peel,
There are waste-paper baskets at the gate.

Pete Stevenson: 2014 / 2018

It was during The Frontline Walk in 2014, that Pete, an RAF Staff Nurse, was staring at the massive structure of the Thiepval Memorial to the Missing. Along with everyone else, he took some photographs of the memorial and started to walk away, but something made him return. Coming from the Nottingham area, he was interested in his local Regiment the Sherwood Foresters and looked for the correct panel on the monument. It was then that he noticed two entries for the name Stevenson on pier 10, along with hundreds of other men from the Regiment.

On returning home Pete soon discovered that his great-uncle Thomas Stevenson had died during the Battle of the Somme. The family had never discussed it and Thomas had been forgotten. Pete discovered that his great-uncle had served in the 2nd Battalion, Sherwood Foresters, and had been killed near Ginchy on 16 September 1916. According to the Commonwealth War Graves Commission records, he had no known grave and was recorded on the Thiepval Memorial. To his amazement Pete noticed that Thomas was remembered on pier 10, the same pier that he had photographed during The Frontline Walk. He quickly looked at his photograph and there it was, a photograph of his great-uncle's entry on the memorial!

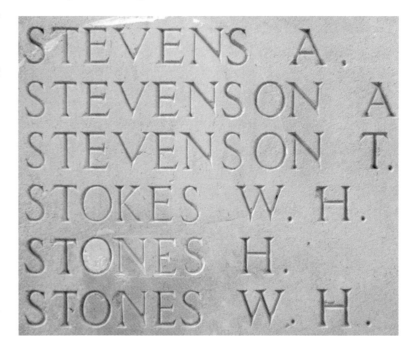

The name of Thomas Stevenson on the Thiepval Memorial to the Missing.

On 16 September 1916 Thomas and the Sherwood Foresters were heavily involved in the fighting near Ginchy. During a four day period they were attacking a heavily defended German strongpoint known as 'The Quadrilateral', so called because it had four sides and was heavily fortified with machine guns. Thomas was one of 654 casualties from the Battalion during the four days 1916.

Since The Frontline Walk in 2014 Pete has returned to the Somme on several occasions and, in 2016, he used the 2nd Battalion's war diary to find the very location where Thomas had been killed.

Jane Tutte: 2016 / 2018

In 2015 Jane, from Cornwall, was privileged to be invited to work with a lady whose father-in-law had served in the Red Cross during the First World War. She had a collection of his letters, written to his wife during the war and she helped her transcribe them and put together a timeline of his movements. One day she found herself holding a letter where he described witnessing the arrival of the first tanks and their deployment during the Battle of the Somme. He described their impact and how he felt this could surely change things now. Jane was touching history. Inspired by all this, she decided to learn more and visit the Western Front herself. She saw the perfect opportunity to do this by signing up to The Frontline Walk in 2016.

Whilst Jane knew the walk would be physically challenging she was not prepared for the emotional challenge. She was not aware of any relatives that died in the war but that didn't diminish the impact it had on her. Jane takes up the story:

"As I walked my thoughts turned to my own ancestors. Both my grandparents had fought and had survived. My paternal grandfather was Private Thomas Henry Tooth, 2/5th Battalion East Lancashire

Top: Jane crosses the finishing line at the Menin Gate in Ypres.

Regiment who according to the family had a shortened finger on his left hand, an injury sustained in the war. However, due to the fantastic research of one of the walk historians, his story came to light. I now know when he joined, where his Battalion fought, where he sustained the wound and the damage that was done. It must have been a considerable injury to his hand as the records show that he was in hospital for five months. Thomas Henry Tooth was one of the lucky ones who came home but he died before I was born. My maternal grandfather, Gunner Charles Walter Perry, served in 242nd Brigade, Royal Field Artillery. My mum told me that he worked with the horses that pulled the guns and that he never spoke of his time there, so that was all the information I had. Charles lived until he was aged 94. His soldier's records were lost during the Second World War so his story couldn't be told. However, I did know him and, when I think about it now, it saddens me greatly that I never once spoke to him about his time as a soldier. Even if, as my mother had said, he didn't want to speak of his experience and what he had endured, I could have let him know that I cared and that I was so incredibly proud of him for serving his country. It is a regret that can never be remedied but the one thing I can do is go on remembering."

Stuart Wilkie: 2016 / 2018

By marriage Stuart is related to brothers Albion and Frederick Caldecourt. The brothers served together in the Essex Regiment during the First World War. *"I found out about the brothers from a member of the family when the British Legion ran a campaign to remember all those who had fought and paid the ultimate sacrifice."* Stuart explained:

"As I was taking part in The Frontline Walk in 2016 I found that this was the perfect way on behalf of the family to pay our respects and to remember them. I was very lucky that Terry, one of the other walkers, offered to do some research about the brothers for me. With Terry's hard work and interest he sent back a very detailed record for both brothers and the approximate location of where they fell and on what date they died, Albion on 1 July 1916 on the Somme and Frederick on

Despite the number of visits I have made to France and Belgium I always come away with a feeling of how proud I am of these men and boys.

15 September 1916, also on the Somme. Having served myself in the Royal Air Force, being able to follow in the footsteps of our brave soldiers who paid the ultimate sacrifice was both an honour and a privilege. I still to this day, after visiting the many areas of the First World War battlefields, cannot comprehend what these brave men and boys put themselves through their bravery, loyalty and sacrifice that they made for their country is remarkable, and I feel that we should remember them today, tomorrow and forever. Despite the number of visits I have made to France and Belgium I always come away with a feeling of how proud I am of these men and boys, and listen to the many stories to enhance my knowledge and have a clearer understanding of what life must have been like to have served on the frontline day after day and seeing your comrades becoming injured or even killed. Being part of The Frontline Walk allows me to pay my respects to all those men and to give back what I can."

Chris Woolsey: 2017 /2018

When he took part in The Frontline Walk, Chris, as a soldier, was well aware of the work of the Charity and the opportunity to give something back to assist former comrades was a big incentive to take part. So too, was the opportunity to follow as closely as possible in the footsteps of one of his relatives who had died on the Somme in 1916. Chris relates his story:

"Sergeant William Shanks served in 11th Battalion, Royal Scots. He had enlisted in late 1915 and after training arrived in France in the early summer of 1916. By July his Battalion was on the Somme battlefield ready to take part in the 'Big Push'. It was early in the morning of 3 July 1916 that William and his Battalion arrived in the village of Montauban, which had been captured on 1 July 1916. A number of patrols were sent out to ensure that there were no Germans still in the area. Throughout the day the area was shelled by the Germans and the Battalion suffered a number of casualties.

The shelling continued throughout 4 July 1916, causing casualties among the units in Montauban and nearby Bernafrey Wood. The 11th Battalion Royal Scots reported the loss of twelve men due to the artillery fire. Three of them had been killed while on a patrol into Bernafrey Wood, although the war diary fails to name these men.

Among the twelve men reported as killed on 4 July 1916 was Sergeant William Shanks. William's final resting place is not known and today he is commemorated on the Thiepval Memorial to the Missing."

A moment of reflection: Chris follows in the footsteps of William Shanks on the Somme.

CHAPTER 7

DAY 2: ARRAS

On the second day the route moved across ground fought over in 1914, 1915, 1916 and 1917. It covered areas initially fought over by the French and Germans and later by British and Canadian troops. Although the day's walking moved across much of the battlefields, it also took walkers through rear areas and the sites of artillery positions, ammunition dumps, and medical units. Day two also introduced walkers to both German and French cemeteries, providing them with the opportunity to reflect on all sides of the conflict.

The day started at first light at the German Cemetery (Soldatenfriedhof) at Neuville-St-Vaast where the remains of over 44,000 German soldiers rest. For many walkers, the opportunity to walk amongst the sea of crosses as the sun came up was an emotive start to the day, and always provoked questions. Leaving the cemetery the route passed 'Maison Blanche Farm' and over the tunnel system, situated below the buildings

Opposite: Colonel Andy Reid views the names on the Arras Memorial.

Left: The battlefield near Arras.

Arras

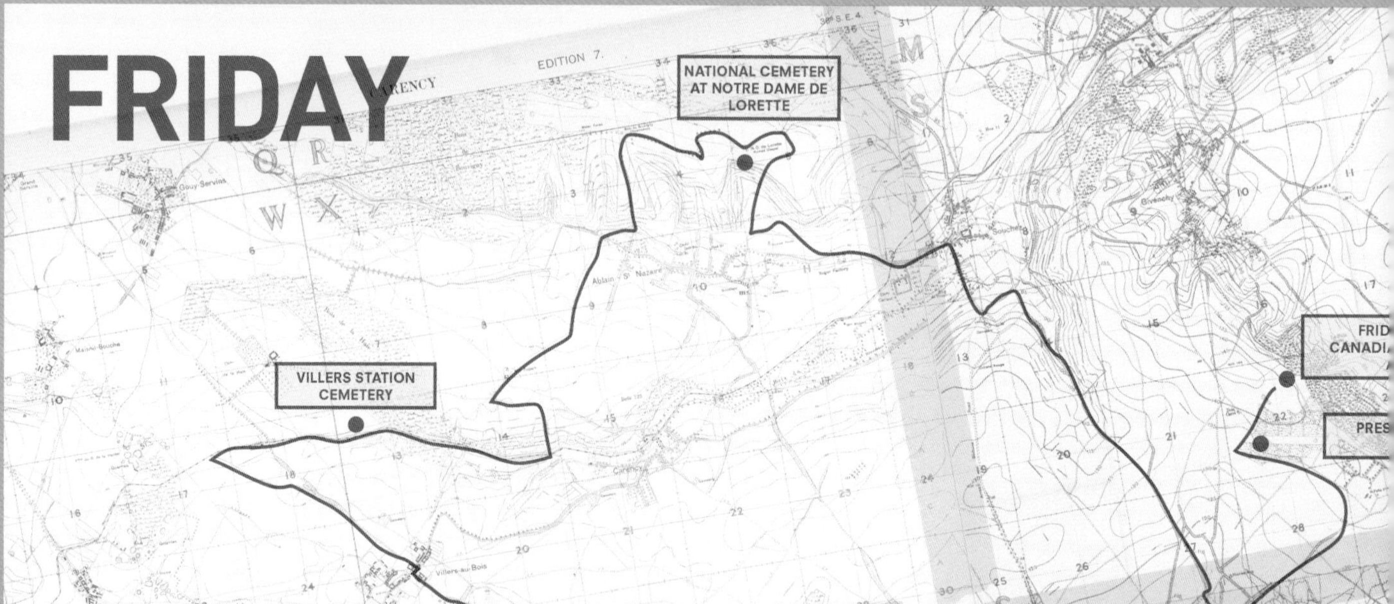

FRIDAY

NATIONAL CEMETERY AT NOTRE DAME DE LORETTE

VILLERS STATION CEMETERY

FRID CANADI

PRES

TOWERS (REMAINS OF OLD MONASTERY) AT MONT-SAINT-ELOI

ECOIVRES MILITARY CEMETERY

FRIDAY – START NEUVILLE-SAINT-VAAST GERMAN MILITARY CEMETERY

BRITISH CEMETERY AT MAROEUIL

Day 2: Friday

Start: The German cemetary at Neuville St Vaast.

Finish: Canadian Monument at Vimy.

Distance: 35km

Highlights:

- Neuville-St-Vaast German Military Cemetery

- La Targette Memorial

- Ecoivres Military Cemetary

- Ring of Remembrance

- Canadian Monument at Vimy Ridge

Moving across country, the walkers passed through fields which, in the first few months of 1917, had been filled with artillery pieces preparing for the forthcoming battle. The route then continued towards the rear areas and the village of Maroueil, passing the small French cemetery and the nearby British military cemetery. In Ecoivres, walkers were able to visit the large British cemetery with 1,728 British and 786 French graves, among which rests William Darbourn a relative of walker Carol Williams.

The morning break was sited next to the ruins of the Abbey of Mont St Eloi, used by both French and British troops as an observation point. Moving off after the break the route continued towards a well-earned lunch. But before walkers were fed, they had to climb the steep slope of the Lorette Spur, a ridge line fought over by the French in late 1914 and early 1915. Some of the walkers found the climb arduous, but on reaching the top they were confronted with the sobering site of the French National Cemetery at Notre Dame de Lorette, where over 40,000 casualties now rest.

After lunch on day two the walkers took the opportunity to visit the cemetery and the adjacent 'Ring of Remembrance Memorial' which always took up some of the lunch break, before setting off on the second half of the day's walking.

Moving down the hill and off the ridge line, the route moved through Souchez, which by 1918 was nothing more than a pile of brick dust. It then ran parallel with A26 auto route and over the ground where the Canadian Corps prepared for the attack on Vimy Ridge in April 1917, before turning back towards the village of Neuville-St-Vaast. The final stage of the day's walk headed towards the top of Vimy Ridge and the finish at the inspiring Vimy Memorial to the Missing. This stunning monument records the names of those Canadians killed in France but who have no identified grave. There are 11,285 names on the Memorial, including walker, Steve Milne's relative, William Milne VC, killed near the memorial site on 9 April 1917.

A hot meal at the front.

Colin Beesley: 2015 / 2016 / 2017 / 2018

Colin grew up not knowing either of his grandfathers. He did know that both had served their country during the First World War. Both survived and were discharged to return home only to pass away within a few years from lung disease caused by the effects of having been gassed.

As a young man Colin decided to join up, although against his mother's wishes, he enlisted in the Royal Artillery. In 2015 Colin saw an appeal by the ABF The Soldiers' Charity inviting people to take part in The Frontline Walk, and for the second time in his life felt that same pull to take part; this time he didn't need his mother's blessing.

Colin created a team of eight walkers, consisting of members from all three branches of the Armed Forces. On the first morning, in pitch dark, the team arrived at the start point at the Lochnagar Crater. Colin takes up the story:

"The scene before us, and the emotions that the area evoked, was beyond anything I had ever experienced before. To look across the crater at the land towards where our lines would have been was incredible, and for the first time I sobbed almost uncontrollably. The rest of that first walk continued in a rollercoaster of emotions, ranging from enjoyment of the company I was with to emotional heartache to tiredness."

Opposite: Colin in Rifle House Cemetery, paying his respects at the grave of Rifleman R. Barnett, Rifle Brigade, killed on 19 December 1914 aged 15.

Colin striding out with fellow walker Irvine.

To look across the crater at the land towards where our lines would have been was incredible, and for the first time I sobbed almost uncontrollably.

"Day two began at a German cemetery and was a contrast from British cemeteries. The incredible sparseness and black crosses was again an emotional experience. From there through to Vimy Ridge and onward the day was exhausting, though it wasn't until we reached the coach that we realised how tired we all felt. Day three was definitely the most emotional day. From the grave of a 15-year-old rifleman (boy), to the site of the Christmas football game, to Hill 60, to the end of the walk at the Menin Gate, our aching feet and emotional bodies broke as we walked through the gate. I have never in my lifetime experienced anything close to that afternoon as myself, and fellow walker John McKnight, stood hugging each other crying with emotion."

Colin was bitten so he signed up for the next three years.

"I have now completed four walks culminating in the Hundred Day Offensive Walk in 2018. To follow in the footsteps of those that pushed the German forces back to the final surrender and to stand by the headstones of our fallen was emotional beyond compare. I had thought the first walk was emotional but it hadn't prepared me for the final push 100 years after the Armistice. I have walked with some 400 people, all of whom are the finest people I know. I thank the The Soldiers' Charity and each one of those walkers over the past four years for the experience of lifetime."

Reverend Paul Critchley: 2016 / 2017 / 2018

In 2016 Paul, the superintendent minister for the North Fylde Circuit of the Methodist Church, decided to take up the challenge of The Frontline Walk. He had reached the age of 40 and his wife had completed the London Marathon for ABF The Soldiers' Charity.

Paul decided to dedicate the walk to 2nd Lieutenant Geoffrey Potts who was killed in action during the Battle of Arras in April 1917, whilst serving with the 17th Battalion, Manchester Regiment. Geoffrey is no relation to Paul, but he had become fascinated with his story after discovering a memorial to him in his church in Fylde, Lancashire: *"I really wanted to know more about Geoffrey and discover what happened to him. He had no living relatives that we were aware of."*

Strolling just strolling,
Paul (centre) undertook
the walk dressed in First
World War uniform.

On the day before the walk began, Paul found himself saying a quiet prayer at the graveside of Geoffrey Potts, a few miles outside of Arras in Northern France. He sunk to his knees in pure emotion and was unable to speak for a few minutes. Finding the grave of Geoffrey meant so much to him.

On 23 April 1917, the Battle of Arras had been going on for nearly two weeks but the allies had not yet captured the formidable Hindenburg Line. The 17th Manchesters were given the task of trying again.

At 4.45am the Battalion moved forward ready for the assault. The men spent the next few hours digging themselves in, but at 9.00am the enemy launched a counter attack which was repulsed with great gallantry and the position maintained. At 2.00pm the enemy attacked again and the Battalion suffered many casualties. At midnight, the Battalion was relieved, having paid a heavy price. Out of 650 men who went into the assault, 360 men were killed, wounded or reported missing.

A sentry in an advanced trench.

An eyewitness of the battle on 23 April 1917 reported:

"The Regimental Sergeant Major R.S.M Coates performed excellent work during the assault, repeatedly bringing in wounded men under shell fire, organising the defence of the frontline trench and finding cover, in a shell hole for the mortally wounded Lieutenant Potts."

87 men died on that day, including Geoffrey who is buried in Wancourt Cemetery. His family must have been heartbroken when they received official notification of his death.

Below left: The telegram announcing the death of Lieuteannt Geoffery Potts whose memorial was located in Paul's church.

Below: Paul at the grave of Lieutenant Geoffery Potts killed at Arras on 9 April 1917.

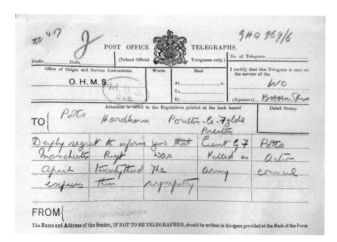

Paul Dunne: 2017 / 2018

With no known relatives serving in the First World War, Paul Dunne, a former soldier, decided to remember a namesake that he found by searching on the Commonwealth Graves Commission website. His chosen soldier was Private Hugh Dunne who came from Ardagh, County Meath and served in the 8th Battalion, Royal Dublin Fusiliers. Hugh went missing during a gas attack at Loos in Northern France on 29 April 1916. His body was never found and he is now commemorated on the Loos Memorial to the Missing.

The 8th Battalion diary described the full horror that Hugh experienced that day:

Paul, left, at the Vimy Memorial.

"At 3.20am the gas attack signal was given again. Two gas clouds settled down on our trench without wind to move it. No bombardment or attack took place and scarcely a man could survive this attack. The casualties from gas poisoning were more severe than on 27th owing to the gas clouds meeting and remaining stationary and concentrated over the trenches. Our casualties over the two days were three Officers killed and 5 others wounded. Other ranks – 81 killed, 53 wounded, 122 gassed, 102 missing. Total casualties for other ranks – 368 leaving a strength of 578."

Paul explained how he felt when he discovered what had happened to Hugh:

"I must admit it's a dreadful feeling to think of him and so many others being gassed. Having served as a British soldier, my career did not end well and I was discharged. For me, the burden and shame has been heavy to carry so I wanted to do something positive to remember the dead and help the living. I enjoyed The Frontline Walk so much in 2017 I did it again in 2018 and have signed up for Normandy in 2019. I take pride knowing the money I raise will help. Having met the Charity's Ambassadors Barney Gillespie and Stewart Harris on The Frontline Walk, they are living proof that we make a big difference to the beneficiaries. The Frontline Walk was a very emotional experience following in the footsteps of so many who did not return, but also very rewarding."

Josh Griffiths CGC: 2014

During The Frontline Walk in 2014, serving soldier Josh Griffiths was looking at the grave of a First World War soldier and he noticed the letters 'MM' on the headstone. "Military Medal" said Josh. Reflecting on what happened to him in March 2013. Josh takes up the story:

"I was getting ready to eat my evening meal at the ISAF patrol base in Nad-e Ali when a pick-up truck driven by a suicide bomber burst through the wall of the base and exploded. The blast left a 40m gap in the perimeter wall – the start of an attack that was to last for several hours. I was wounded by the blast but as Afghan insurgents began to attack the base I fought back to keep them out.

I was thrown around as well as everyone else and the next thing I remember it was dark and I was on my back. I heard one of the lads scream out. I managed to help my colleagues and returned fire, protecting fellow wounded soldiers from insurgents who were spraying bullets at them and throwing grenades, while another attacker was firing rocket propelled grenades from the field outside the base. I stopped the attackers at the wall of the base, and allowed the casualties to be evacuated."

Josh and Terry en route.

It was only afterwards that he realised he had suffered damage to his eye, but during the initial explosion, he had also broken his back. He added:

"I had broken my fourth vertebrae. At the time, when the explosion happened, I thought my back was a bit weird but I heard lads screaming so the job just took over and I pushed forward, treated them and pushed forward again. I think adrenaline kicked in."

The incident that day left one colleague dead and 14 wounded. Josh was awarded the Conspicuous Gallantry Cross for his actions that day but, thinking of his colleague and friend who died that day in Afghanistan. Josh continued:

"It's a great honour obviously to be recognised, but we lost a lad that day so I would rather that hadn't happened than I get the award."

The walk itself was extremely emotive as I come from a family who, through generations, have always served in the military.

John Hallows: 2017

John Hallows, a former serviceman from Northwich, thought to himself "I'd love to do that" when he saw an advert for The Frontline Walk on Facebook. He then discovered that he had a family member who had been killed in the First World War, Private Albert Goddard of the 2nd Battalion, Sherwood Foresters. John was shown a photograph of the Memorial Plaque, which Albert's family had been awarded following his death. These plaques were issued to all the families of the men and women who died in service and later became known as 'The Dead Man's Penny'. It was the inspiration John needed to complete the challenge.

John takes up the story:

"I knew that our great-great-uncle Albert Goddard had been killed and I tried to use various methods of tracing him myself but to no avail. So I set off to France and Belgium unaware of his resting place. The walk itself was extremely emotive as I come from a family who, through generations, have always served in the military. We've had family members in the Infantry, Artillery, Parachute Regiment, Army Catering Corps, the RAF and the Navy.

I found the walk tough but I was in comfortable clothing with comfortable footwear, staying in a hotel after every day of walking and

The name Albert Goddard on the Ring of Remembrance at Notre Dame de Lorette.

The memorial plaque for Albert Goddard, a relative of John's.

I tried to imagine what the men/boys had to endure during the First World War. The stories told by our knowledgeable historians were mesmerising and compelling and you could almost picture the scenario as it was being told to you.

On the second day, we visited the Notre Dame de Lorette Memorial where the ring of remembrance is situated; I searched the beautiful plaques and was able to find the same name on the wall. We ended at Vimy Ridge and I laid a cross of remembrance there. It was a beautiful and very sombre monument for me.

After returning home one of the charity's researchers discovered his name on the Ploegsteert Memorial. I returned to Belgium in October 2018 and travelled to the memorial to pay our families respects. This was all possible thanks to doing the walk, meeting a group of fantastic individuals and enduring a walk, which will stay with me forever!"

Albert had been in France for just six weeks when he was killed on 20 October 1914. The Battalion was holding the frontline trenches at Ettenieres near Armentierres when they were attacked and overwhelmed by a much larger German force. There were just 51 survivors, two officers and 49 other ranks. The Official History reveals what happened:

"The Battalion", wrote Brigadier-General Congreve "had done exceedingly well all day; it was just worn out and overwhelmed by superior numbers." This battalion, moreover, was one which had suffered heavily in action only some four weeks previously, and on October 20th not a single Company was commanded by the officer who had led it a month previously, while only two of the original platoon commanders were left with their platoons.

The number of non-commissioned officers and men killed, wounded and missing totalled 710 and the estimated number of other ranks captured at 484, many of whom were wounded, leaving others killed and wounded."

Steve Milne: 2015 / 2016 / 2018

Steve Milne first learned about the First World War at school. He takes up the story:

"I was fascinated and drawn in by the teacher Mr Drake describing how the men of the York and Lancaster Regiment nicknamed the 'Sheffield Pals' attacking at Serre on the first day of the battle, 1 July 1916 and of the huge numbers of casualties and of the heroism shown that day.

Still drawn to history and the military, at the age of 17 I joined the Territorial Army as a member of the Royal Army Medical Corps. It was a few years later whilst visiting my dad's family in Scotland that I got the chance to speak to Robert Drummond, my great-uncle. He had enlisted aged 17 in the Black Watch and served as a sniper on the Western Front. As we talked he opened up, telling me of his experiences and what life was like in the trenches; fascinated, I learned how he had been awarded the Croix de Guerre. He also told me about a distant family member who he said had been awarded the Victoria Cross.

Many years later on a battlefield tour I went to Vimy Ridge, and while looking at the names of the missing on the Vimy Memorial I saw the name WILLIAM JOHNSTONE MILNE, the relative my great-uncle had mentioned.

William Johnstone Milne had emigrated to Canada in 1901 and found work in Saskatchewan. He enlisted in the 46th Canadian Infantry Battalion in

Above: Steve's relative William Johnstone Milne VC killed in action on 9 April 1917 at Vimy.

Left: The care of feet was always important a foot inspection in the trenches.

Keeping up morale.

September 1915 and arrived in France in June 1916. He saw action during the Battle of the Somme, but it was at the Battle of Arras on 9 April 1917 that he would win the Victoria Cross. As the 46th Battalion attacked near the village of Thelus, they became pinned down by machine gun fire and it was then that William decided to do something about it. He crawled forward on his hands and knees and managed to knock out the first machine gun, killing the crew, and then moved on to the second gun which he also destroyed. Killed later that day he has no identified grave and is now commemorated on the Vimy Memorial.

I've completed The Frontline Walk three times, walking to remember both Robert and William, one who survived and one who didn't. The Soldiers' Charity is now very close to my heart and I raise funds even when not participating in the walks. For the walkers the emotions of being together for a few days after meeting as complete strangers only days before are amazing. For me it is like the military family which will stay with you forever. It's a sense of belonging and of doing some good for those who have served and now, for whatever reason, need help. It's why I walk, why I raise funds to help ex service personnel.

So for Robert Drummond my great-uncle who survived and William Milne who didn't, a distant relative on my dad's side, R.I.P., gentlemen. You did your duty."

Striding out through
Bourlon Wood.

Sandra Patterson: 2017 / 2018

Mental health nurse Sandra Patterson, from Birmingham, completed The
Frontline Walk in 2017 walking in the footsteps of her relative Private 7947
Syrenius Patterson, 6th Battalion, British West Indies Regiment [BWIR],
without even realising it!

The formation of the BWIR did not give soldiers from the West Indies
the opportunity to fight as equals alongside white soldiers. They were
instead largely deployed on manual labour tasks such as road repairs and
the movement of supplies. Their deployment in these supporting roles
intensified as the war progressed, particularly in times of extensive activity.
During the Battles of the Somme, Arras and Passchendaele for example,
casualties among fighting troops meant that reinforcements were needed

at the front. The use of BWIR troops on labour tasks released other troops for the frontline.

A total of 397 officers and 15,204 men, representing all Caribbean colonies, served in the BWIR. Of that total, 10,280 (66%) came from Jamaica. Sandra is of Jamaican heritage, as was Syrenius.

On 25 April 1917, Syrenius was serving at Neuville-St-Vaast, close to where Sandra started day two of The Frontline Walk. The camp was isolated because of an outbreak of mumps and measles. The Army was clearly worried about typhus as everyone was inoculated before they proceeded to Poperinghe, just behind the Ypres battlefield, on 24 June 1917. During the fighting in Ypres in the summer of 1917, Syrenius and his comrades were involved in supporting the infantry. They were not, however, out of danger suffering a number of casualties during the battle.

On 14 January 1918, Syrenius and his comrades arrived in Marseilles and were billeted in tents. Four days later Syrenius was admitted to hospital. The only document Sandra could find in his service record revealed that he was seriously ill on 4 May 1918. It reveals he was suffering from "Tuber on the lungs" – Tuberculosis. He died just ten days later. He probably contracted the disease on the Western Front, in the dreadfully wet and muddy conditions of late 1917. He was laid to rest in Mazargues War Cemetery in Marseilles.

Above: Sandra visiting the grave of Syrenius Patterson in Marseille.

Opposite: Sarah Pylyp at the grave of Private Talbot Burch in Dozingham Cemetery.

Sarah Pylyp: 2017

When Project Manager Sarah Pylyp from Coventry bought a British Legion poppy pin little did she realise how it would affect her. The pin came with a card remembering a soldier chosen at random from the battlefields of Ypres. Her named solider, Private Talbot Burch, served with the 19th Battalion, Durham Light Infantry and had died of wounds on 4 November 1917.

As one of the top fundraisers on The Frontline Walk in 2017, Sarah was one of those chosen to lay a poppy wreath at the Menin Gate on the last evening of the walk. Sarah takes up the story:

I was thinking about all of the mothers whose sons didn't come home. I was also trying to hide the tears that were streaming down my face.

Sarah laying a wreath on behalf of the charity at the Menin Gate.

"I was thinking about all of the mothers whose sons didn't come home. I was also trying to hide the tears that were streaming down my face. Finally, I was hoping I wouldn't fall flat on my face on the cobbles in my high heels! It was such a proud moment in my life."

The previous day Sarah had been reduced to tears of emotion during a visit to a massive German cemetery near Vimy Ridge – "these young lads are somebody's sons", she said at the time, whilst wiping away the tears. She was also thinking of the German soldiers as she laid the wreath.

Talbot Burch came from Sheffield and, before the war, was helping his parents manage a pub. By 1916, he was actually managing the pub, but on 16 May 1916 his younger brother Percy was killed on the Somme and it was only four days later on 20 May 1916 that Talbot joined up. Perhaps he volunteered in order to avenge his brother's death?

In October and November 1916, shortly after joining his battalion on the Somme battlefield, Talbot was involved in holding the line in terrible conditions. In April 1917 the Battalion was involved in the Battle of Arras where on one single day, 23 April 1917, they suffered over 264 casualties.

In October 1917 Talbot and his Battalion arrived on the Ypres battlefield. By then the 3rd Battle of Ypres was well advanced and the autumn weather had turned the battlefield into a muddy death trap. At 8.00am on 27 October 1917, the 19th Battalion started the long and difficult march from the reserve areas north of Ypres to the support line at Pascal Farm.

The Battalion War Diary reveals that a single shell dropped on 'D' Company and caused "a considerable number of casualties". On 10 November 1917, without entering the frontline trenches or taking part in an attack, the Battalion was withdrawn from the line. During the period they had suffered terribly from shellfire, gas and sickness and it was at some point during this time that Talbot must have been wounded.

A telegram from the War Office confirmed that Talbot had died of his wounds at No 61 Casualty Clearing Station. Talbot now rests in Dozinghem Cemetery where Sarah was able to visit his grave after completing The Frontline Walk.

Pauline Tovey: 2017 / 2018

Harry Haycock was born on 4 January 1898. His age, did not however prevent him from serving his country during the First World War. Lying about his age, he enlisted in the Territorial Army on 26 September 1914 giving his age as 17 he joined 2/7th Battalion, Worcestershire Regiment as Private 2724, a genuine "Boy Soldier".

By April 1915 Harry had been promoted to Lance Corporal and as a Territorial Soldier had volunteered to serve overseas. He arrived in France with his battalion in May 1916. Initially all went well for him, but in September 1916, Harry was admitted to hospital suffering from shingles. He remained there for seven days before re-joining his unit.

Army life clearly suited him and his continued progress as a soldier was recognised with the award of the 'First Good Conduct Badge'. Worn as an inverted stripe on the left cuff, the award recognised good conduct during service in the Army. It could be awarded to Privates and Lance Corporals who had been of good conduct for two, six, twelve or 18, years.

Harry and his battalion spent the last few months of 1916 on the Somme battlefields. Despite the fighting drawing to a close, and the bitterly cold weather conditions, trenches still needed to be occupied. As such, Harry and his mates spent four days over the Christmas period, surviving the harsh winter conditions in 'Regina Trench' near Courcelette.

During 1917 Harry together with his battalion moved north to take part in several attacks during the 3rd Battle of Ypres, now more commonly known as Passchendaele. During their time in the area the battalion suffered heavy casualties through artillery fire and, on one occasion, a gas attack. It was during the closing stages of the battle that Harry chose to relinquish his Lance Corporal's stripe and reverted to the rank of Private.

In late October 1917, Harry was admitted to hospital with pains in his legs and arms. He was evacuated back to the United Kingdom and a hospital in Blackpool diagnosed as suffering with 'Trench Fever'. During the three months he remained in this hospital he was treated with massage and also electricity, which doctors believed would relieve the symptoms.

After being discharged as fit and after a short period of leave Harry returned to France in September 1918. It seems that he was not however fully recovered, and within a few weeks he had reported sick and again

Pauline's grandfather, Private
Harry Haycock, a survivor.

been returned to the UK; he was subsequently medically
downgraded and discharged from the army.

His conduct sheet remained clear of any charges and
he died aged 90 in 1988.

29 years after his death, his granddaughter Pauline
Tovey, from Kidderminster, took part in The Frontline Walk
in honour of her much loved grandad. Pauline explained:

*"Gran and grandad Haycock looked after me before
I started school when my parents were at work.
He played bowls several times a week. He also
umpired local cricket matches. Although he was
active socially he wasn't 'social' and always seemed
remote. I thought of grandad a lot on the walk,
trying to understand the man he was, and I think I
did. No-one sees the things he did, at such a young
age without it leaving scars."*

Richard Walton: 2016 / 2018

Richard Walton, from Taunton, has fond memories of his great-uncle
Alfred. He remembered, as a small child, Alfred showing him how to swing
a cricket bat. Like so many others, Alfred didn't talk to Richard about his
experiences as a Captain during the First World War. Nor did he mention
that he returned to France in 1940 and took part in the Dunkirk evacuation.

Before the war Alfred was employed as a solicitors' clerk, and as a middle
class professional man he was clearly suitable for military service. Joining
the Territorial Army, he was commissioned on 16 December 1912 as a 2nd
Lieutenant in 2nd South Midland Brigade, Royal Field Artillery [RFA]. Following
the outbreak of war Alfred was mobilised into full time service as a Lieutenant
in 241, Brigade RFA, and arrived in France in April 1915. He was promoted to
Captain in October 1915, just six months after arriving on the Western Front.

By June 1916, 241 Brigade were located on the Somme and took part in
the bombardment that preceded the Battle of the Somme. He was wounded
in action on 24 July 1916. The Brigade Diary for that day records *"activity
at night on communications"*. At the time he was serving as a Captain in

'C' Battery and was probably wounded by shellfire. He was sent to hospital on 26 July 1916, although his wounds cannot have been too serious, as three months later he re-joined the unit.

By March 1917 Alfred had been appointed as the Adjutant within 241 Brigade. As such he was responsible for the production of the Brigade's war diary on behalf of the Commanding Officer. The diaries provide a daily record of the unit's activities and this role was fulfilled by Alfred for a number of months, the entry in March 1917 for example, were certainly signed by him.

He clearly did not remain at Brigade Headquarters, as two entries in the *London Gazette* reflect his courage under fire. On 19 November 1917 the Gazette records the award of the Military Cross to Alfred. The citation read:

> *"For conspicuous gallantry and devotion to duty. He carried out a most valuable reconnaissance for a forward observation post. Later, although twice wounded, he continued to command his battery with great energy and ability, bringing it to a very advanced position through very difficult ground. His courage and cheerfulness set a fine example to all ranks."*

A single line entry on 4 February 1918 records that Alfred was awarded a Bar to the Military Cross, effectively a second award, although it provides no details.

Alfred served until the Armistice and was transferred to the reserve of officers in 1919. He clearly enjoyed military life and opted to remain in service and following a number of promotions commanded 241 Brigade between 1924 and 1931.

He also served throughout the Second World War, being evacuated from the beaches of Dunkirk in 1940. Richard takes up the story:

> *"At Dunkirk he marched his men off the beach. When they reached the small boat he took off his helmet and put on his artillery cap with a red flash so his men knew the boss was waiting for them!"*

Captain Alfred Hobson was a natural leader of men.

Top: Richard's great-uncle Alfred with the officers of 2nd South Midland Brigade Royal Field Artillery.

Above: The Medal Index Card for Alfred Hobson

Carol Williams: 2016 / 2018

In 2016 Carol Williams turned 50 years of age and decided to celebrate this milestone by walking 1,000 miles and raising money for charity. She entered various events, and then saw The Frontline Walk being advertised on social media.

Carol's family were always aware of a great-uncle, William Darbourn, who had died in the First World War, and she decided to take on the challenge of the walk to celebrate her life milestone and the short life of William. Carol explained:

"I didn't know anything about my great-uncle until 2004, when my husband suggested that I put my surname into the Commonwealth Graves website to see what came up (I have an uncommon maiden name). I didn't know that the walk was going past the cemetery where his grave is, when I saw that it did I felt so humbled and honoured to be taking part in the walk."

Wellington Barracks and time to meet old friends.

British Royal Artillery officers of the 9th Division examining a German 5.9 inch howitzer captured in the west bank of Happy Valley, during the Battle of Arras.

William's unit, 5th Canadian Mounted Rifles [5 CMR] arrived in France in September 1916 and were almost immediately sent to the Somme where it took part in the successful attack on the village of Courcelette. With the onset of winter William spent five days in hospital with bronchitis.

On Easter Monday, 9 April 1917, the four Canadian Divisions fought together as the Canadian Corps for the first time. Taking part in the Battle of Arras they were given the job of capturing Vimy Ridge. William and his comrades in 5 CMR were an integral part of this attack.

Prior to the battle deep tunnels had been dug, allowing the assaulting troops to move to their jumping-off points without being seen by the Germans. The tunnels protected the men both from shellfire and the weather: they also permitted the wounded to be brought back from the battlefield. William and his mates entered Goodman tunnel system the day before the planned offensive. It had piped water and was lit by electricity provided by generators.

Leaving the tunnel the men moved into their jumping off trench 'Albany Avenue' and at 5.20am, advanced across 'No Man's Land' towards a German trench called 'Swischen Stelling'. The Germans, aware of the attack, as part of their defences had positioned 40 men in shells holes in front of their trenches. These men immediately opened fire causing a number of casualties among the advancing Canadians, one of whom was William. He

THE TOWN SQUARE, ARRAS, FRANCE. FEBRUARY, 1919.

Above: Town square, Arras 1919.

Opposite: William Darbourn.

was recovered from the battlefield and evacuated the short distance to a Field Ambulance located at Ecoivres for medical attention. He died there the following day.

Carol explained how she felt when she discovered his grave, at the place where he had died:

"As we passed the beautiful cemetery where he now lies, I was so overwhelmed to think that I was the only member of his family to have visited his grave in 83 years. On my return the Charity's researcher discovered what had happened to William and I felt so much closer to a relative that had been lost to our family for so many years. In 2017 I was lucky enough to attend the 100 years memorial of Vimy Ridge service and also lay a wreath at the Menin Gate on the 100th anniversary of his death."

CHAPTER 8

DAY 3: YPRES

The third day of the walk, set in the Ypres area, started with an early departure from Arras and the drive north to Belgium. Between 2014 and 2016 the Ypres day started at the Hyde Park Memorial to the Missing at Ploegsteert and moved towards the finish line in Ypres itself.

In 2017, to mark the 100th anniversary of the Third Battle of Ypres (Passchendaele), it was decided to start north of the city and to walk as much of the 1917 Salient as possible. This was repeated in 2018.

The 3rd Battle of Ypres or, as it is more commonly known 'Passchendaele', provides people with the typically accepted images of the First World War;

Opposite:
The Menin Gate.

Left: A lunar landscape in 1917, craters at St Eloi.

Ypres

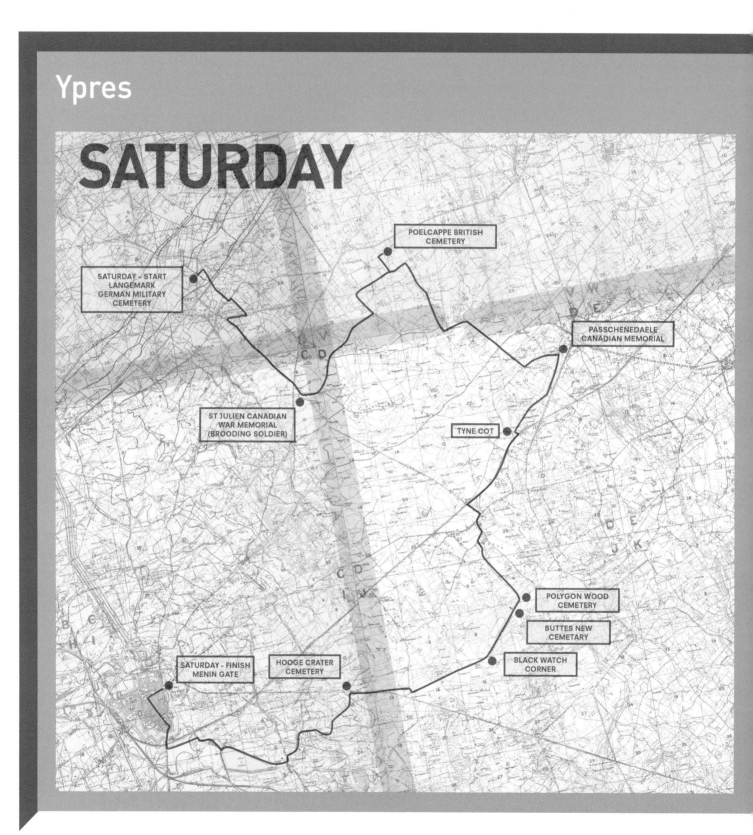

SATURDAY

POELCAPPE BRITISH CEMETERY

SATURDAY – START LANGEMARK GERMAN MILITARY CEMETERY

PASSCHENEDAELE CANADIAN MEMORIAL

ST JULIEN CANADIAN WAR MEMORIAL (BROODING SOLDIER)

TYNE COT

POLYGON WOOD CEMETERY

BUTTES NEW CEMETARY

BLACK WATCH CORNER

SATURDAY - FINISH MENIN GATE

HOOGE CRATER CEMETERY

Day 3: Saturday

Start: Vancouver Corner.

Finish: Tyne Cot Cemetary.

Distance: 31km

Highlights:

- St Julien Canadian Memorial

- Poelcapelle Cemetery

- Tyne Cot Cemetery – world's largest Commonwealth War Cemetery

- Polygon Wood

- Buttes New British Cemetery

- Black Watch Corner

- Menin Gate

impressions of a featureless landscape marked by water-filled shell holes and devastation, with men simply disappearing into the mud. The battle which commenced on 31 July 1917 was fought by the British 2nd and 5th Armies and continued until 10 November 1917. The intention of the offensive was to breach the series of German defensive lines around Ypres and in doing so allow an advance towards the northern Belgian ports.

Leaving the German Cemetery at Langemark, the walkers moved towards the Canadian Memorial to the gas attacks at 'Vancouver Corner' and then on towards the British Cemetery

A German bunker in Flanders similar to
the three visible in Tyne Cot Cemetery.

at Poelcapelle and the morning break. As the route moved over the ground
many walkers found it was difficult to imagine the horrors experienced by
men struggling through the waterlogged landscape. For the walkers, the
carnage was clearly illustrated when they arrived at the morning break next
to Poelcapelle British Cemetery where over 6,000 of the graves are unknown.

Moving towards the village of Passchendaele the route passed such places
as 'Varlet Farm' and 'Crest Farm' before turning and following the old railway
line back towards Ypres and Tyne Cot Cemetery. As they walked through the
headstones in Tyne Cot, walkers looked towards the city of Ypres and out
over the battlefields, fought over in August and September 1917. The route
continued along the old railway line towards Zonnebeke, and the lunch
break was taken in the grounds of the Passchendaele Memorial Museum.

Leaving the lunch site, the route headed towards Polygon Wood. The trail
moved through the wood and past the German pillbox, now known as 'Scott's
Post', before arriving at 'Black Watch Corner' and the memorial recording the
regiment's actions in November 1914. The afternoon break was located on the
Menin Road, close to 'Hooge' Cemetery, and the walkers then moved on to
Zillebeke Lake and the final meeting point, which again was located at a bar.

Once all the walkers had gathered and after a short respite, the group
set off on the way into Ypres. As they walk through the 'Lille Gate' and
into the town, the walker's spirits were always high, particularly when they
were greeted and applauded by the people of Ypres as they passed the bars
and shops. Heads were raised, shoulders went back and the efforts of the
previous days were forgotten as the group passed under the Menin Gate
and through the finish line.

Tony Benham: 2015 / 2017 / 2018

After his father died in November 2014, Tony wanted to continue the research his father had started into his grandfather, Private 201498 George Johnson of the 9th Battalion, King's Royal Rifle Corps. Tony takes up the story:

"On Remembrance Day 2014 dad was very ill and I bet him a fiver that we would get him out of hospital for the ceremony. I won and I still have the fiver in my wallet today!"

Tony wanted to find out more about his great-grandfather's experiences, and perhaps even follow in his footsteps on the battlefields.

Detailed research revealed that George had seen action at Delville Wood and Guedecourt during the Battle of the Somme, and that his Battalion had lost hundreds of casualties. This was George's first experience of the war on the Western Front, but not his last.

In April 1917 George was in action during the Battle of Arras, when his Battalion attacked a formidable German strongpoint known as 'The Harp'.

Top: Tony reflects at the memorial to the Kings Royal Rifle Corps on the Menin Road, Ypres.

The attack was successful and they captured 200 Germans, half of them pulled from the dugouts in the enemy trenches. Success came at a terrible cost though, with 214 men either killed, wounded or missing.

In August 1917 the 3rd Battle of Ypres was in full swing and George was holding the line, with his comrades, close to 'Chateau Wood' along the infamous Menin Road.

They fought the Germans for three long days and suffered another 138 casualties in "desolate" and "swampy" conditions. On the final section of The Frontline Walk in 2017, Tony was reduced to tears when he discovered a memorial to the King's Royal Rifle Corps which was positioned on the very spot where his great-grandather spent those three dreadful days 100 years earlier. Tony said:

"I couldn't believe it. I knew he served somewhere there but to stand on the very ground where he fought was incredible. I only wish my dad was there with me but, in a way, he was. I will never forget that moment."

Below: Tony in the centre of a wreath laying party at the Menin Gate.

Following pages: Tony points out his relative's name.

ALBE...
PRIVA...
BENHAM G.
BUCKOKE W.
CHAMBERLAIN E. A.
CHAPPELL W. G.
CORNWELL J.
CRAKE S. G.
CURRIE W. T.
GOODMAN F. E.

LONDON

BN

LCE CORPORAL
MORLEY H.

RIFLEMAN
AUGUST A. E.
BARNETT M.
BLACKMAN E.
BURNS E. A.
COLE J. G.
DANIELS H. J.
FINCH W.
KENDALL C. E.

LIEUT

WOOD

REGIM...
RIFLE...
LEWIS
LOKAT...
MACK...
PERR...
REES...
ROB...
SEE...
TA...
T...
T...

Laura Bowkett: 2016

Private James Olley, 2nd Battalion, Duke of Cornwall Light Infantry, was one of 72 men blown to pieces by a German underground mine at a location called 'The Mound', a few miles south of Ypres. Like most of the men who died in the explosion, James has no known grave and is commemorated on the Menin Gate Memorial in Ypres. An eye witness described the events that day:

"At 5.30 pm, whilst I was gazing towards the Mound, I suddenly saw the trench there lifted into the air; sandbags and debris seemed to rain around, and a moment later there came a dull 'boom' of the explosion. At the same instant the whole German line opened fire; away by the Mound I saw the enemy advancing. We immediately opened fire on our front. I remember firing my revolver at two men; whether I hit them I know not; in fact I have no clear recollection of what did happen for several minutes."

It was 101 years later in 2016, that his descendant Laura Bowkett, from Milton Keynes, passed 'The Mound' on the final stages of The Frontline Walk. Laura takes up the story:

"My mum works for the charity and she told me about The Frontline Walk. I have a number of family members who have been in the Armed Forces, including my stepfather and my grandad. I wanted to learn more about the First World War and raise money for the charity and, luckily for me, my friend Jenny Baulk agreed to join me on the walk, and I am so glad she did as I couldn't have done it without her!

The pain I encountered on the walk was insane. Even though my feet were used to my boots because of my training, I still had blisters on blisters. No amount of tape helped on the second day, so unfortunately I was advised by the doctor to not continue the last six or so miles. 'Gutted' was an understatement! Waiting for Jenny to get to the finish on the second day at Vimy Ridge was a mixture of emotions for me.

I wasn't going to let the blisters stop me from completing day three though. And I didn't. I have never felt pain like it. There were tears, anger and laughter from us both! The other walkers encouraged us when we felt low and it helped both Jenny and I. We were not going to give up!

The moment when we walked up the cobbled street towards the Menin Gate was crazy. My feet were so, so heavy and I could have easily stopped. When the public started clapping us... Oh my God! The tears started pouring. I remember us looking at each other and we realised we had completed the challenge. Seeing all the graves, memorials and hearing all the stories was so amazing. I cried a lot but I also laughed a lot. I will never forget the whole experience."

Laura, on the extreme right, leading the group on the final stage towards Ypres and the finish line.

On 11/11/18 or on becoming non-effective		Rank	NAME	Unit previously served with. Regtl. No. and Rank in same on entry into theatre of war	Theatres of war in which served					
Regtl. No.	Rank				From	To	From	To	From	To
G/38859	Pte		OLLEY JAMES	11th RWS.G/38859 Pte a|4|17 ✓						

635758 | 88326 | Olley James. | 11th Bn R.W.Surrey Regt. death Pte Resumed 38859 | 18/7 Hounslow 2d | 5 | 19 7 | 5 19 7 | No.4 18 | 10.4.19 Fa Herbert | 5. 19 7

A.F.W. ... DATE 10·4·19

WAR GRATUITY. Transfer 19/20 Feb 65 20 3.19 Regd. Paper 3.6 20 20 Dec 88 Serial No. 15163.

3 | 10 | | 5.1.20 Fa Herbert | 3 | 10 — | PN

Documents relating to James Olley.

Z

Name.	Corps.	Rank.	Regtl. No.
OLLEY	11. Queens R.	Pte	6/ 38859
James.			

Medal.	Roll.	Page.	Remarks.
VICTORY	E/1/101 B15	2895	
BRITISH	—do—	—do—	
STAR			
Theatre of War first served in			
Date of entry therein			K. 1380

DUKE OF CORNWALLS LIGHT INFANTRY. _____ REGIMENT OR CORPS.

ROLL OF INDIVIDUALS entitled to the Victory Medal and/or British War Medal granted under Army Orders 266 and 301 of 1919.

772 (b)

On 11/11/18 or on becoming non-effective		NAME	Unit previously served with. Regtl. No. and Rank in same on entry into theatre of war	Theatres of war in which served								Clasps awarded (to be left blank)	Record of disposal of decorations (a) Presented (b) Despatched by Post (c) Taken into Stock	REMARKS
Regtl. No.	Rank			From	To	From	To	From	To	From	To			
21207	Sgt	OLIVER. JOHN.	6/DCLI.21207.SGT 1/DCLI.21207.											
37096	Pte	OLIVER. JOHN GREGORY.	1/4.DCLI.37096.PTE											
240410	Pte	OLIVER. JOSEPH.	1/5.DCLI.2550.PTE 1/5.DCLI.240410. 1/DCLI.240410.											
34669	Pte	OLIVER. LOUIS.	6/DCLI.34669.PTE											
41163	Pte	OLIVER.LEWIS EDWARD	1/DCLI.41163.PTE											
27517	Pte	OLIVER. RUEBEN.	2/DCLI.27517.PTE											
260062	Pte	OLIVER. SAMUEL.	1/DCLI.260062.PTE 1/DCLI.260062.											
9040	Pte	OLLEY.JAMES HENRY.	2/DCLI.9040.PTE											
18431	Pte	OLSEN. PERCY HENRY.	1/1.DCLI.18431.PTE											
28877	L/Cpl	OLVER.CHARLES ROBERT	1/5.DCLI.28877.A/SGT 7/DCLI.28877.											
19234	Pte	OLVER.EDWIN JOHN.	6/DCLI.19234.PTE att/10.Ent.Bn.19234. 6/DCLI.19234.											
8870	Cpl	OLVER. ERNEST.	2/DCLI.8870.A/SGT 7/DCLI.8870.											

I certify that according to the Official Records the individuals named in this ROLL are entitled to the Medal or Medals as detailed above.

Place _____ EXETER.

Date _____ APRIL 1920.

Signature and rank of Officer certifying.

| 635758 | 488326 | Olley James. | 11th Bn. R.W.Surrey Regt. Pte Presumed 38859 | 1/8/7 Hameland 2/8 Death Presumed | 5 | 19 | 7 | | 5 | 19 | 7 | Nov.4.18 | 10.4.19 J.a.Herbert | 5 | 19 | 7 |
| | | | WAR GRATUITY. Transfer 19/20 Regd. Paper Serial No. | | 3 | 10 | | | | | | | 5.1.20 J.a.Herbert | 3 | 10 | |

A. F. W. ... DATE 10.4.19

Documents relating to John Olley.

Campaign :— 1914-15.	(A) Where decoration was earned. (B) Present situation.				
Name	Corps	Rank	Reg. No.	Roll on which included if any	
(A) Olley	D of Corn L.I	Pte	9040	V. 101. B9. 772	da / da
(B) J.H. Lives	"	"	"	8	C/1/4/13 28
Action taken			Pres.ᵈ Dead		
THEATRE OF WAR.	(1) France		68/121/995		
QUALIFYING DATE.	19.12.14				

(6 34 46) W234—HP5590 500,000 4/19 HWV(P240) K608 [OVER.

Will Carver: 2018

In May 1915, 19-year-old student Graham Adam decided to enlist in the Canadian Army. Having completed his basic training, he arrived on the Western Front in October 1916 and joined the 31st Infantry Battalion. A few months later he was wounded in the face but, after a period of convalescing in the UK, he returned to his unit in time for the 3rd Battle of Ypres, often known as the Battle of Passchendaele.

On 6 November 1917, his unit successfully attacked the village of Passchendaele; despite the success, casualties were heavy. Graham was one of 300 casualties suffered by his unit in what was one of final days of the battle. His body was lost and he is remembered today on the Menin Gate Memorial in Ypres.

After he was killed, his father wrote this painful letter about Graham:

"We used to hear regularly from Graham from "somewhere in France." He used to write very amusingly and pluckily. He was wounded in the face and was sent to the base hospital, where he was marked "P.B." which meant "Permanent Base." We were very relieved at this as it meant he would never return to the frontline. Alas, about this time the 'Passchendaele offensive' took place and every available man was sent up. On Nov. 6th, 1917 we got a telegram to say Private Graham Adam of the 36th Battalion (he had been drafted from the 56th) was missing. We made every possible enquiry through Hubert Man and others but never heard any trace of him, so presume he must have been blown up by a shell in that terrible campaign. Dear boy, he was anything but warlike and must have hated trench life and

Pte Graham Adam, Will's distant cousin killed at Passchendaele in 1917.

Everybody seems to wish that the war was over, even the troops themselves say so. I wish it were over too, and cannot get up much enthusiasm for killing, or being killed (especially the latter).

all the horrors of war, but was very, very plucky and must have done well as he was a company-runner when he met his end. His name is on the Menin Gate at Ypres."

27 April 1915, whilst suffering from measles:

"Everybody seems to wish that the war was over, even the troops themselves say so. I wish it were over too, and cannot get up much enthusiasm for killing, or being killed (especially the latter). Some of the men indulge in the most gloomy thoughts: 'it's no use you thinking about ever going back to Canada,' they say, 'because you're not going back'."

Tragically, he never returned home to Canada; 100 years later, Graham's descendant, Will Carver from Alaska, remembered the sacrifice of his distant cousin by completing The Frontline Walk. Like so many others, Graham has no known grave but will always be remembered by his family.

Elly Clark: 2016 / 2018

Following the death of her grandfather, Elly's mother decided to look at the family tree. It was then that Elly first discovered that she had a great-great-uncle called Bertie Ambrose and that he had been killed during the First World War. *"My mum asked my gran if there were any photos of Bertie"* explained Elly. Her gran replied that there was one somewhere but she had no idea where.

"During a search of the attic, mum and dad found several boxes of family memorabilia, pulled one randomly towards them, blew off the dust and opened the lid. There, on the very top of the pile, was Bertie – possibly the only photograph ever taken of him, taken just before he went to war. It felt like he had been waiting for us to find him. He stares straight into the camera, young, chin tilted, proud of himself and determined, but his eyes betraying a little trepidation about what lay ahead for him.

I had signed up for The Frontline Walk and the training before the walk helped me, giving shape and reason to my own life. I looked up where

Bertie was buried and was told I would be able to visit his grave on my walk. This became the focal point of my trek. On the third day when I was due to leave a copy of the photograph on his grave, I misplaced it and was absolutely heartbroken. After searching everywhere again, I managed to find it; the sense of relief was incredible.

Giving a face and individuality to that clean uniform grave mattered hugely to me. Steve the Historian and Ed the photographer accompanied me to Bertie's grave in Messines Ridge British Cemetery. I was surprised that I felt nervous as I walked towards it. I had no idea why. I was meeting my 19-year-old relative, who had been dead for a century. I laid a poppy together with the copy of the photograph at his grave. Now anyone who walked past would know his face and see that he had been remembered.

There was the culmination of the walk for me – the end, through Menin Gate, was hugely emotional as we all cried and hugged each other. But that still quiet moment in Messines cemetery with my ancestor was for me what all the months of training, pain and fatigue had really pointing towards. I reached back into the past and held my uncle's hand."

Elly puts her best foot forward for the cause.

▶▶

I laid a poppy together with the copy of the photograph at his grave. Now anyone who walked past would know his face and see that he had been remembered.

◀◀

Elly at the grave of great-great-uncle Bertie in Messines British Cemetery.

Left: Pete, left, enjoys a well earned midday break.

Below: Pete and Karen at Vimy Ridge Memorial.

Pete Cracknell / Karen Cracknell: 2017

For many years, firefighter Pete Cracknell travelled to the Western Front with his parents. His father Andrew had served in the Royal Military Police, and on leaving the Army served with Essex Police as a Traffic Officer. Tragically, Pete's father died suddenly in 2008 after suffering a cardiac arrest.

Pete had always tried to keep the battlefields close to the family following Andrew's death, visiting a handful of times, not only for his enjoyment but as a nod to his father. When Pete saw The Frontline Walk advertised, he knew that his dad would have signed up immediately, so there was no question; as he couldn't, Pete would. When he mentioned his idea to his mother (Andrew's wife) Karen, she also signed up. Pete suffered some good-natured banter from fellow walkers when they discovered he was travelling with his mum.

Pete was in the second wave of Red Watch Firefighters to attend the tragedy at Grenfell Tower. Although not much was spoken about nor mentioned on the walk, Peter did mention that the long days walking gave him time to reflect, to think and put things in perspective, something that he admitted he needed.

Right: Pete, a serving fireman, attended the Grenfell Tower tragedy.

Below: A former British Army hut, now used by returned Belgian refugees on the Ypres-Menin Road, 1919.

*The fact that out of the thousands
of people that support The Soldiers'
Charity ... that on my walk, my dates,
two people knew dad, it gave me a
huge smile inside, and still does.*

Pete's dad, Andrew who
introduced him to the
Western Front who sadly
passed away in 2008.

On the 2017 walk, there were a few RMP veterans walking in the
group, including the historian Steve Roberts. Pete overheard one of
the 'Red Caps' on his phone saying *"You'll never guess whose son
I'm walking with, Andy Cracknell's, Crackers."* Pete says:

> *"That really made me feel like dad was there. The fact that out
> of the thousands of people that support The Soldiers' Charity,
> and the years of walks that had been done, that on my walk, my dates,
> two people knew dad, it gave me a huge smile inside, and still does."*

Andrew had been researching a relative who had been killed at Ypres
in August 1916 but sadly he never got to finish it. Pete asked one of the
charity's researchers to find out what had happened to Private 19767 Henry
Cracknell of 2nd Battalion, Hampshire Regiment. Pete and Karen were
amazed when they discovered that on day one of the walk the route passed
the very spot where Henry's battalion had been, during the attack on
Beaumont Hamel on 1 July 1916 during the Battle of the Somme.

Later in July 1916 the battalion moved to the Ypres area, and on the
evening of 8/9 August 1916 they were in trenches near Potijze when the
gas alarm sounded. Carried by the wind, it took an hour for the gas cloud
to pass over the British trenches, and for the air to clear. Despite the men
wearing gas hoods which helped protect them, many still succumbed to the
effects of the heavy concentration of chemicals which still penetrated their
gas hoods. This resulted in 125 men dying of gas poisoning, 60 of them,
including Henry are buried together in Potijze Chateau Lawn Cemetery.

Pete and Karen finished their time on the Western Front the way they
have always finished it, with a visit to Potijze Chateau Lawn Cemetery to
pay their respects to Henry and his comrades.

Clare at the
reconstructed trenches
at Vimy Memorial.

Clare Crouch: 2016 / 2018

Completing The Frontline Walk meant that Clare Crouch, a Director of
HRS Creative in Lewes, was walking in the footsteps of her relative James
Crouch, who served in 5th Battalion, Royal Sussex Regiment, during the
First World War.

James' battalion was a 'Pioneer Battalion'. An early solution to the
vast demand for labour each infantry Division had a dedicated 'Pioneer
Battalion', trained and capable of fighting as infantry, but normally engaged
on labouring work within the Divisional area. They were responsible for
labour tasks such as road repairs, construction of storage areas and other
labour tasks, often working under the orders of the Royal Engineers. They
would also be responsible for the Divisions equipment such as picks and
shovels and other technical stores.

ROYAL SUSSEX ——— REGIMENT OR CORPS.   3496/B. Royal Sussex Regt.

ROLL OF INDIVIDUALS entitled to the Victory Medal and/or British War Medal granted under Army Orders 266 & 301.   of 1919.

On 11/11/18 or on becoming non-effective		NAME	Unit previously served with. Regtl. No. and Rank in same on entry into theatre of war	Theatres of war in which served								Clasps awarded (to be left blank)	Record of disposal of decorations (a) Presented (b) Despatched by Post (c) Taken into Stock	REMARKS
Regtl. No.	Rank			From	To	From	To	From	To	From	To			
240959. ✓	Pte.	FENTON, Reginald, William.	3405.1/5th.R.Suss.R. Pte. 240959.1/5.R.Suss.R.											
240960. ✓	Pte.	LE.BRETON, Ewart, John.	3410.1/5th.R.Suss.R. Pte. 240960.1/5.R.Suss.R.											
240961. ✓	Pte.	CROUCH, James.	3413.1/5th.R.Suss.R. Pte. 240961.1/5.R.Suss.R.											
240965. ✓	Pte.	BAKER, William.	3419.1/5th.R.Suss.R. Pte. 240965.1/5.R.Suss.R. 240965.9th.R.Suss.R.											
240966. ✓	Pte.	GUHR, William.	3420.1/5th.R.Suss.R. Pte. 240966.1/5.R.Suss.R.											

I certify that according to the Official Records the individuals named in this ROLL are entitled to the Medal or Medals as detailed above.

Place The Barracks, HOUNSLOW.

Date   4 OCT 1920

Lieut. Colonel i/c Record Office. Hounslow.
Signature and rank of Officer certifying for

The Medal Roll entry for Clare's relative James Crouch.

Although not normally involved directly in the fighting, their work was often on or near to the frontline and was still very dangerous, and they could be called upon in the event of an emergency or other shortage of manpower.

On the eve of the battle of the Somme, James' Battalion was near Colincamps. In preparation for the coming battle a number of mass graves were needed, one of which was near Colincamps. Perhaps James was one of those involved in digging the pit?

1 July 1916, the opening day of the battle, was for the most part a disaster. At Serre, the 31st Infantry Division's attack had been thoroughly beaten and it was there, during the following two weeks, that James' Battalion was positioned. The men were involved in repairing the trenches, clearing the ground which included removing and burying the dead, and digging new trenches. This work was completed whilst being fired on by enemy artillery and heavy losses were incurred.

By June 1917, the Battalion had moved to the Ypres Salient in Belgium, ready to play its part in the 3rd Battle of Ypres, more commonly known as Passchendaele.

The battle commenced on 31 July 1917 and 5 Royal Sussex was very soon involved in supporting the attacking forces. The Battalion had already suffered casualties with the War Diary stating that 100 men had been admitted to hospital during the previous month with "gas symptoms".

During August 1917, the battalion was based in various locations on the Pilckem Ridge, a few miles east of Ypres. Casualties during the month were described as "numerous but not serious in nature, except on 16 August 1917. Reinforcements badly needed as effective working strength getting very low. 2 platoons having effectively disappeared". On 16 August 1917, a major attack took place near Langemarck.

On 4 October 1917, the Battalion moved into positions on the canal bank near Boezinge. Very soon after this and probably whilst repairing a road or trench, James was wounded and transferred to a Casualty Clearing Station [CCS] at Dozinghem. Located eight miles from Boezinghe and away from enemy shelling, it was at Dozingham that he died of his wounds on 7 October 1917. He was laid to rest in the cemetery adjacent to the CCS.

Barbara Hocking: 2017

Barbara, a retired Midwife/Nurse and now an artist from Mevagissey in Cornwall, completed The Frontline Walk in memory of her grandfather, Sapper Edwin Marsden Collings, Royal Engineers and her great-uncle, Petty Officer Charles E. Strevens, Royal Navy. Barbara takes up the story:

"As soon as I read about The Frontline Walk, I connected with the sadness and great loss of the First World War to families throughout the UK. I created a Facebook page and my family and friends were amazingly generous to the charity helping me raise £2,740.50! It was very humbling because times are very hard for the villagers, but they all had relatives who had served in the First World War. It was very daunting leaving home arriving at Wellington Barracks to travel with strangers, and be welcomed so warmly helped so much."

Edwin survived the war but, like many others, he got himself into trouble during basic training. He was confined to barracks and lost one days' pay after being late back to barracks because he was 'courting' a young lady! He had a close shave in action as he was wounded in the arm by a shell fragment and spent 60 days in a British Army hospital in France.

Charles joined the Royal Navy in 1905, serving in the China Seas before the outbreak of the First World War. After the Armistice he was assigned as

a Petty Officer to the Dreadnought class battleship, HMS *Superb*, sailing to the Black Sea to supervise the transfer of Russian made ships that had been used by the German Navy.

Even before the war had ended another tragedy struck the world; an influenza pandemic that would kill millions of people worldwide, more than the war itself.

The pandemic spread rapidly, causing high death rates in previously healthy people. The close confines of life on board ship proved an ideal breeding ground for the virus and even Royal Naval battleships were not exempt. Shortly after arriving on the Black Sea, Charles became ill and he died on 8 December 1918, a month after the war had ended.

Charles was buried in Sevastopol Russian Cemetery along with six other British servicemen. The cemetery was destroyed by the Germans in the Second World War and no longer exists. The men buried there including Charles, are now commemorated on the Commonwealth War Graves Commission, Haidar Pasha Memorial in Turkey. Barbara's father is named after Charles, so his memory lives on in her family.

"I felt the deepest connections for me with my grandfather and great-uncle. The small Cornish village that had sponsored me, and all the encouragement and support they had given me, made me connect with all those men volunteering for war, far from home. And why I would walk every step and more, to complete this wonderful challenge."

Above: HMS *Superb* in the Mediterranean, leading the British Fleet to Constantinople, November 1918.

Below: Barbara's great-uncle Petty Officer Charles Strevens who is commemorated on the Haidar Pasha Memorial to the Missing in Turkey.

Laying the wreath at the Menin Gate with fellow walker Phil Morris.

Kirsty Laird: 2015 / 2017

Kirsty Laird, from Exeter, completed The Frontline Walk twice in memory of her great-great-grandfather, Corporal Frederick Harry Laird of the 1st Battalion Bedfordshire Regiment. At the emotional end of the 2015 Walk, Kirsty became the first family member to visit the Menin Gate and lay a wreath in his memory.

At the outbreak of war in August 1914, Frederick was a regular soldier and took part in the early engagements. He fought at Mons and at the Battle of the Marne where he was slightly wounded. Sent to a base hospital, he soon recovered from his injury and re-joined his unit in time for the 1st Battle of Ypres.

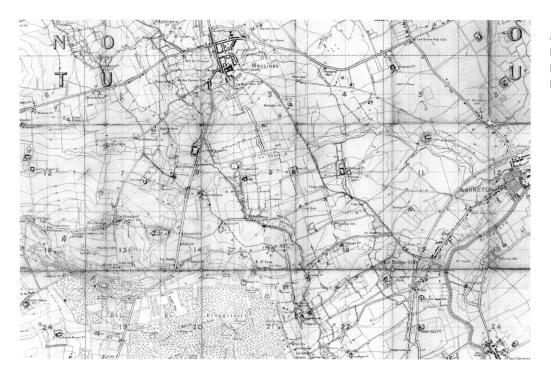

A trench map of the Messines area where Frederick Laird was killed in December 1914.

Between 7 November 1914 and 19 November 1914, the Battalion formed part of the defence of Ypres; holding out against repeated German attacks against the British lines, they remained in what was to become known as the Ypres Salient. Taken out of the line for a rest, the battalion moved back to Locre. During the rest period, Frederick wrote to his mother:

> "*I have been made Corporal for twice going in front of the firing line about 500 yards and fetching wounded men into safety and for digging out Sergeant Box who got buried with a shell at Ypres, under heavy fire, after being slightly wounded myself in the ankle. I have a lot to tell you when I get home which I hope will be soon.*"

On 10 December 1914, the Battalion was back in the line opposite the village of Messines. The war diary states:

> "*Patrols and scouts reconnoitred German trenches during early morning and found Germans alert and trenches protected by wire. Casualties 2 killed and 3 wounded.*"

One of the two men killed was Corporal Frederick Harry Laird. Both men are still recorded as missing in action with no identified burial location. Frederick is commemorated on the Menin Gate Memorial to the Missing.

Tragically, Frederick died before he could return home and see his son, Frederick Harry Laird junior, born on 11 January 1915.

I plan to take George to the Menin Gate and the old battlefields, as soon as he is old enough, so that he too can see the resting places of the many that fought and lost their lives in the First World War and pay his respects to Frederick.

German prisoners being marched through Ypres after the Battle of the Menin Road. Ruins of St Martin's Church dominating the centre background.

Shortly after returning from her second Walk, Kirsty discovered she was expecting her first child. Her son George was born in August 2018.

Kirsty feels very strongly about remembering her ancestor and passing on his memory to George:

"After having my own child, and with the centenary of the end of the First World War approaching and making plans for Remembrance Sunday, I have thought recently what a miracle it is that we are here as with my great-grandad being born in the January. He must have been conceived not too long before the outbreak of war. I have also thought how tragic the news must have been for his wife Julia. During conversations with my late grandmother she told me that her grandmother never got over the loss of her son Frederick.

I plan to take George to the Menin Gate and the old battlefields, as soon as he is old enough, so that he too can see the resting places of the many that fought and lost their lives in the First World War and pay his respects to Frederick."

Steve Marchant: 2018

On the final day of The Frontline Walk in 2018, Steve Marchant was exhausted and looking forward to the climax of the trek at the Menin Gate in Ypres. The route took him through Polygon Wood and along a quiet road, typical of so many around Ypres. If Steve could have turned the clock back to 11 November 1914, he would have seen his great-uncle Herbert Marchant being wounded and taken prisoner close to the spot where he was standing.

Private 5288 Herbert Marchant, a regular soldier, served in 1st Battalion, Scots Guards. He had enlisted aged 16 in 1904 and after three years transferred to the reserve in 1907. With War declared on 4 August 1914, Herbert was recalled to the colours and reported for duty on 5 August 1914.

With his battalion, Herbert arrived in France in September 1914 and, in October and November, was present during the 1st Battle of Ypres as the British Expeditionary Force [BEF] attempted to prevent the approaching German Army from surrounding and capturing the city of Ypres.

By 10 November 1914, the Scots Guards had been fighting day and night for three weeks and were worn out, half fed, unshaven and in rags. They were in the fortified buildings of 'Northampton Farm'.

The exhausted soldiers of the BEF made the most of a quiet night, unaware it was the lull before the next storm was unleashed on them. Withdrawing thousands of exhausted troops and replacing them with fresh reserves, the German 6th and 4th Armies intended to make one last attempt to break the Allied line around Ypres. They were to attack the next morning around Polygon Wood and further south, just where 1st Scots Guards were resting.

The following day, 11 November 1914, approximately 200 survivors of the battalion were entrenched in and around 'Northampton Farm', just north of the Gheluvelt Road. The War Diary records

"Terrific shelling commenced at 6.30am and lasted for 3 hours, all trenches and dug outs were knocked in."

Above: POW card of Steve's great-uncle Herbert Marchant captured near Ypres in 1914.

Opposite: Walking into Ypres.

The shelling was followed by massed infantry attacks with the Prussian Guard leading the assault. The Scots Guards faced the greatest weight of the attack and they were very quickly overwhelmed. Unable to hold back the enemy the British line was pushed back. The men of the Scots Guards in forward positions became isolated, having to fight hand-to-hand to push their way back. The German advance got to within 200 meters of the British artillery lines before the attack was stopped and driven back.

It was during this action, on 11 November 1914, that Herbert was wounded and captured by the Germans. He spent the rest of the First World War in a German Prisoner of War camp, although he was able to regularly correspond with his family via the Red Cross. Steve said:

"The family thought that he had escaped from captivity in August 1918 but there is no mention of it in the records. But I was amazed to discover I had visited the place where he was captured, without even realising it."

Sara McCann: 2017

In 2017, Sara McCann and her mum Heather Perry, from Edinburgh, completed The Frontline Walk in honour of her great-grandfather Lance Corporal William Brough who served with 9th Battalion, Black Watch. Whilst researching his story, Sara discovered a newspaper report that explained how his mouth-organ tunes were immortalised in a poem by popular Dundee soldier-poet Joseph Lee.

The poet changed the name of the man behind the mouth-organ to Jimmy Morgan to help his verse rhyme, but always acknowledged that the best player in the battalion was Willie Brough. The newspaper account says the Black Watch soldier had displayed a *"perfect genius"* for the mouth-organ since boyhood and that he *"cheered his comrades in billet and in battle"*. It says he lightened "many a weary and trying hour" with his music, especially Scottish tunes, reminding the troops of home.

On the eve of the 3rd Battle of Ypres, more commonly known as Passchendaele, William's battalion began moving up to the assembly trenches, ready to advance at dawn on the following day. But William did not take part in the advance. He was the only one in his unit killed on

Above: Sara and her mum Heather pause at the Black Watch Memorial near Polygon Wood.

Below right: The obituary notice for William Brough, Sara's great-grandfather and the poem by Joe Lee.

He was killed on the very first day of Passchendaele and in one way I'm glad he was killed at the start.

30 July 1917; he was probably killed by German shellfire, but we will never know for certain.

The Battalion Diary records that as the men moved forward into 'Cambridge Trench' they suffered two casualties, one man was killed and the other wounded. William was probably buried close to where he fell but his body was lost and he is now commemorated on the Menin Gate Memorial in Ypres, along with over 54,000 others who perished on the Ypres battlefields and who have no known grave.

William, who was married with four children, had joined the Army in 1914 and seen two years of service in France before Passchendaele. He had fought both on the Somme in 1916 and at Arras in April 1917.

The newspaper account of Willie's death ends with the hope that his fabled mouth-organ would be placed among Dundee's war relics. Unfortunately, neither Willie, nor his mouth-organ were ever recovered.

Sara and her family had already visited the place where William died and they decided to take part in The Frontline Walk in his honour. Sara felt very emotional walking in the footsteps of the relative she never met:

"From what I know of the battle it was hideous. People were drowning in the mud because of the rain. It was just the most awful time. He was killed on the very first day of Passchendaele and in one way I'm glad he was killed at the start."

She says the story of his mouth organ playing "brought him to life" for her and other relatives because it told them about his personality. Sara says:

"What I love most about him is that even in those circumstances, which were hideous, he was able to keep his spirits up and lift others as well."

CHEERED OUR LADS IN BILLET AND BATTLE.

DEATH OF "JIMMY MORGAN."

Lance-Corporal William Brough, Black Watch, known to Dundee lads at the front as "Jimmy Morgan," has fallen in his country's cause. The lance-corporal from boyhood displayed a perfect genius in playing the mouth-organ, and when he went on active service he and his humble instrument were continually in requisition. Many a weary and trying hour he lightened with his music. He was the original of "Jimmy Morgan" in one of Joe Lee's "Ballads of Battle":—

Sometimes he pipes us grave hopes,
Sometimes he pipes us gay;
Till broken feet
Take up the beat
Of quick-step or strathspey;
But he plays upon our heartstrings
When he plays a Scottish tune,
Hear Jimmy Morgan
And his old mouth-organ
At "The Banks o' Bonnie Doon."

And now Willie Brough has gone to join many another brave lad in the Great Beyond, and the music with which he cheered his comrades in billet and in battle will be heard no more. I trust his little instrument has been preserved, for when we in Dundee come to gather together our war relics Willie Brough's mouth-organ should certainly have a place among them.

When I woke up that morning I had no idea that Samuel Rudge even existed. Now there I was, close to where he died 100 years ago, feeling such strong emotions for a man I didn't even know.

Darren and the 'Rugby Relics' raising yet more money for the charity as they walk and sing requests.

Darren Parker: 2017

Darren served in the Royal Military Police. In Iraq during the 1991 conflict, he had a narrow escape himself when, without realising, he drove through a minefield and came out on the other side unscathed. In 2017, Darren and his former comrades Andy and Chris were reunited for The Frontline Walk. On the third morning, Darren received an email from his aunt in New Zealand. She asked him to keep a look out for his ancestor Samuel Rudge, who was apparently buried "somewhere on the Western Front".

Incredibly, two hours later Darren was paying his respects to Samuel at Tyne Cot Cemetery. The cemetery on the Passchendaele battlefield, is now the final resting place of nearly 12,000 Commonwealth soldiers who perished in the First World War. It is the largest Commonwealth Cemetery in the world. Darren was almost overcome with emotion – *"it was incredible"* he explained:

> *"When I woke up that morning I had no idea that Samuel Rudge even existed. Now there I was, close to where he died 100 years ago, feeling such strong emotions for a man I didn't even know."*

Further research revealed that Samuel was killed by shellfire less than a mile from where he is now buried. It was one of the "quiet" days on the battlefield, with just five men from his Battalion killed. His body was initially buried by his comrades where he fell but was exhumed and reburied in Tyne Cot Cemetery in September 1919, two years after he died. There he lay, almost forgotten, until Darren came along on a cold October morning and ensured that Samuel Rudge will always be remembered.

Darren at the grave of his ancestor Samuel Rudge in Tyne Cot Cemetery.

Chris Price: 2017 / 2018

As a Military Policeman, Chris served in Northern Ireland, Bosnia and both Iraq conflicts. He was inspired by the story of his relative, Thomas Travers, who aged 40 served in 2nd Battalion, King's Shropshire Light Infantry. He arrived in France in February 1915 but was killed only two months later on 13 April 1915.

Four men of the battalion died that day; three of them, including Thomas, have no known grave and they are now commemorated on the Menin Gate Memorial to the Missing, in Ypres. The local newspaper in Shropshire reported on his death:

Top: A few years service.

"Whitchurch has made a splendid response to the call to arms and many of her gallant sons have already given proof of that British pluck and determination that will eventually result in crushing Prussian militarism. In this life and death struggle Shropshire has to deplore the loss of many sons, and one of those who have nobly given his life to King and Country is Private Thomas Travers, 2nd Shropshire L.I.,

Right: In the tank cemetery outside Ypres. This house is a typical farm house of the region during the reconstruction, made entirely from material salvaged from the trenches.

Below: Chris's relative Thomas Travers, killed in April 1915.

Below right: The name of Thomas Travers on the Menin Gate.

PRENTER J.   TILL J.
PRICE A.   TOWNSEND G. J.
PRICE C.   TRAVERS T.
PRICE H.   TREGUNNA F.

I felt immense pride because I realised that a member of my family had fought so valiantly but had paid the ultimate price. It was very evocative seeing his name up there, and then I noticed my own namesake on the same panel!

*whose home was at
Barlow's Yard, Whitchurch,
and who was killed in
action on April 13th being
shot whilst engaged in
digging a trench and dying
almost immediately. Private
Travers was in his 40th year
and a bag maker by trade;
he joined the Shropshire's
in September, and had been
with the 2nd Battalion in
France since February 1915.
He was married, and leaves
a widow and four children,
with whom the greatest
sympathy is felt."*

British soldiers laying
a light railway line
near Boesinghe,
Belgium, July 28, 1917
during the Battle of
Passchendaele.

His widow received this letter:

*"Private Thomas Travers had been killed on the 13th digging trenches
at the time, and was shot in the stomach, dying shortly afterwards in
practically no pain. He was a very good soldier and I am very sorry
to lose him. Deepest sympathy is felt with the widow and children in
their bereavement."*

– Lieutenant L.J.B. Lloyd

Chris spoke of his feelings about discovering Thomas on the Menin Gate:

*"As I walked the battlefields I felt humbled and emotional but then,
at the end of the Walk, I saw Thomas' name on the Menin Gate and
I felt immense pride because I realised that a member of my family
had fought so valiantly but had paid the ultimate price. It was very
evocative seeing his name up there, and then I noticed my own
namesake on the same panel! I had to find out what happened to
Thomas, which I did within a couple of weeks of returning home. The
whole experience has made me want to become a battlefield guide
and share his story with others. It has changed my life forever."*

Martin Shepherd: 2016 / 2018

The First World War, and The Frontline Walk, often throw up stories of tragedy, sadness, pain and sorrow. Occasionally, a happy story comes up out of the horror of the trenches. When Hugh Shepherd, serving with 6th Battalion, Manchester Regiment was gassed and wounded near Ypres in 1917, he could easily have been another of the sad stories. But fate was to have its say, and 100 years later, his grandson Martin Shepherd, following in his footsteps, walked across the battlefields, in memory of not just Hugh, but a young nurse called Annie.

In September 1917, the 3rd Battle of Ypres, more commonly referred to as Passchendaele, was in full swing and conditions for the combatants were getting worse and worse, as the rain continued to fall on the smashed landscape of Flanders. Casualties on both sides mounted and it was a struggle just to stay alive as so many troops were lost, many drowning in the mud and flooded shell holes.

Hugh's Battalion were ordered to attack several ruined farm buildings on the 'Frezenberg Ridge', which had been turned into heavily fortified

Above: Hugh Shepherd who was gassed near Ypres in 1917.

Right: Annie the nurse who treated and later married Hugh standing in the rear row third from the left.

positions, reinforced with concrete. During the action, Hugh suffered from the effects of gas poisoning and was evacuated to a Casualty Clearing Station well behind the lines. From there he was moved to a large Base Hospital before being transferred back to the UK. At some point along the way he was cared for by a nurse called Annie. No doubt many young, wounded soldiers became very fond of their nurses, but in this case the feelings were reciprocated and Annie and Hugh fell in love. They married, had children and years later Martin himself was born. Without the horrors of the battlefields, Hugh and Annie would never have met and Martin would not have been born.

Naturally, Martin is forever grateful to his grandparents and their First World War service. Their love story inspired him to complete The Frontline Walk in 2016 and again in 2018.

"The walk is always an emotional event even if you do not have family who served, but in both Flanders and the Somme I walked in my late grandfather's footsteps so it was even more emotional for me."

Soldiers creating a home from home, when all about them there is nothing but waste and ruins.

CHAPTER 9

THE HUNDRED DAYS OFFENSIVE

The Last Hundred Days

The 11 November 2018 marked the 100th anniversary of the end of the First World War. To commemorate this, The Soldiers' Charity decided to mark this historic event. For 2018 only, a unique walk took the walkers over the northern French battlefields of the last one hundred days of the war. For the walkers and the historians this proved a challenge, moving away from the more traditional trenches of the Western Front and a route which moved over large areas with very little to see. Although the events and stories are still there, the cemeteries are far fewer and further apart, the more easterly the route moved.

Opposite: After travelling from London, walkers visit the Arras Memorial as a first stop.

Below: Information panels placed along the route for the walkers.

Day 1

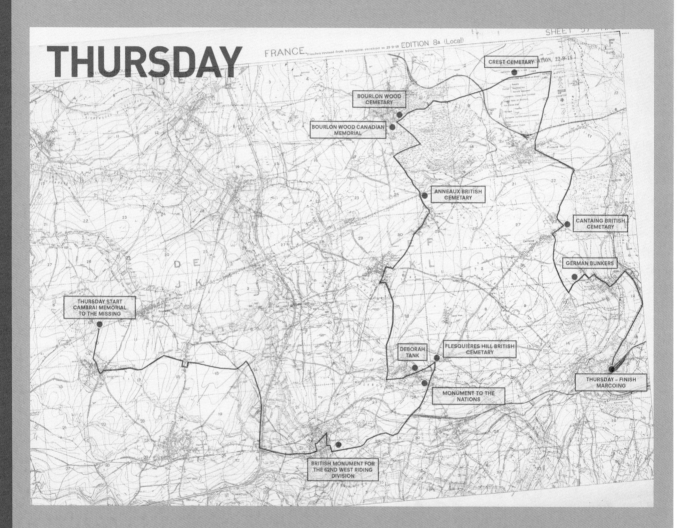

Thursday

Start: Cambrai Memorial to the Missing

Finish: Marcoing

Distance: 36km

Highlights:

- Monument to the Nations

- Deborah Tank

- German Bunkers at Noyelles

On the first day, walkers gathered at the Louverval Memorial to the Missing of the 1917 Battle of Cambrai. Setting off the walkers moved in a loop towards Havrincourt and then crossed the Canal du Nord, as the Guards Division had in September 1918. Following the route of the Guards battalions, the walkers moved on to the village of Flesquieres and the morning break. The group were extremely fortunate during the morning break, when local historian Philippe Gorczynski arranged a visit to the First World War tank 'Deborah', now housed in her own museum in the village.

Walkers were able to visit British Tank, 'Deborah' during the morning break.

Day 2

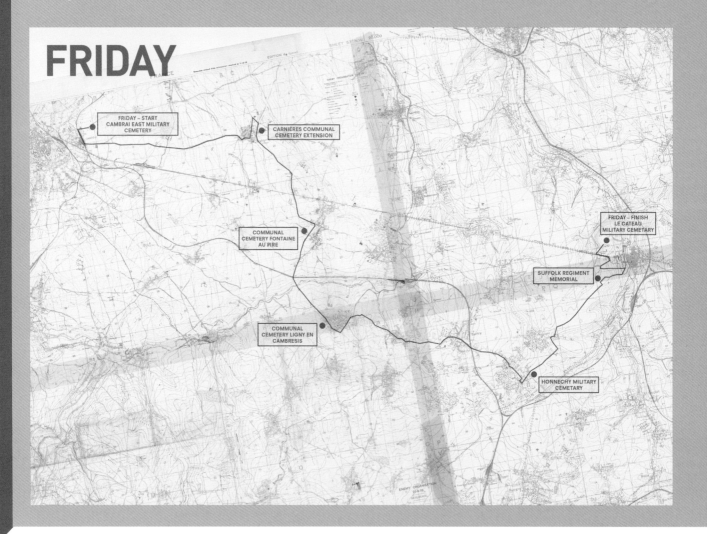

Moving away from Flesquieres the route took the walkers north and into the depths of Bourlon Wood, captured by Canadian forces in September 1918. On the far side of the wood the walkers were able to stop for lunch before setting off for the afternoon. Following the advances of September and early October 1918, the walkers continued on towards the day's finish point on the far side of the St Quentin Canal at the village of Marcoing.

The second days walking started at the Cambrai East Military Cemetery, which contains both German and British casualties. For many walkers, day

Friday

Start: Cambrai East
Military Cemetery

Finish: Le Cateau
Military Cemetery

Distance: 36km

Highlights:

- Honnechy Military
  Cemetery

- Le Cateau Battlefield

- Suffolk Memorial

- Le Cateau Military
  Cemetery

two proved to be the hardest, in terms of walking, as the route moved east away from Cambrai across wide expanses of farmland with very little to see. Passing through quiet villages, with only the occasional points of interest combined with hard tracks under foot, very warm weather made the going hard. There were, however, highlights such as the village of Carnières, where the Mayor put on his ceremonial sash and greeted the walkers to his village. The discovery of British soldiers graffiti on the local church was also of interest. As the route passed through the 1918 battlefields it also moved across the area of the 1914 Battle of Le Cateau, and the discovery of both 1914 and 1918 casualties in cemeteries proved particularly poignant for some. Among the casualties at Honnechy British Cemetery, for example, lay nine men who had died exactly 100 years ago to the day of the walk.

The route for day two continued across ground which, in 1918, had few trenches and saw the fighting move into mobile warfare, moving quickly over the area. The finish point for the day was located at Le Cateau Military Cemetery, which again contains a number of nationalities including British, German, French and even Russian soldiers.

For the final day of the walk, the start point was situated next to the Roman ruins in the village of Bavay. The village had also played a part in the 1914 campaigns when the British Commander Sir John French established his headquarters there prior to the Battle of Mons. For historian Steve Roberts, Bavay took on a personal interest when he discovered that his grandfather, Private Henry Goddard, spent the night in the town on 7 November 1918, before continuing the advance, the following day.

Leaving Bavay, the route moves north east towards another pivotal episode in British Military history when it passes through the village and 1709 battlefield of Malplaquet. By this point in 1918, the German Army was retreating rapidly with allied forces pursuing them. Despite this, there were still large numbers of casualties, as German units fought rear guard actions. This is reflected in the random groups of Commonwealth War Grave Commission headstones spread amongst the many village communal cemeteries along the route towards Mons. For example, Nouvelles Communal cemetery

Day 3

contains four men of the Royal Naval Division who, having been wounded on 10 November 1918, died of wounds the following day.

On approaching the outskirts of Mons, the walkers gathered at a hostelry a short distance from the finish. Once gathered, the group set off for the final stretch towards the Military Cemetery at St Symphorian. A cemetery originally created by the Germans, it now contains individual plots for both German and British casualties. As a finish line for the Hundred Days Offensive walk, a fitting site was chosen with walkers

Saturday

Start: Bavay Roman Ruins

Finish: Saint Symphorien Military Cemetery

Distance: 28km

Highlights:

- Saint Symphorien Military Cemetery

- Bavay

- Malplaquet

- Nouvelles Communal Cemetery

- St Symphorian Military Cemetery

Another day and more respects to pay.

passing between two individual headstones. On the right that of Private John Parr, 4 Battalion, Middlesex Regiment, killed on 22 August 1914, the first British soldier killed in action and on the left, that of Private George Ellison, 5 (Royal Irish) Lancers, killed in action at approximately 9.30am on 11 November 1918, the last British soldier to be killed in action.

'The First and the Last'

Sharon and Mike Anthony: 2017

Able Seaman Frederick Cyril Driffill of the Royal Naval Division [RND] was one of the many, killed during the last few weeks of the war. Frederick, more commonly known as 'Sid', came from Goole and had been a slater in civilian life.

He had served at Gallipoli and on the Western Front throughout the conflict, and he must have thought he was going to get through the war unscathed.

In late September 1918 the Germans were in full retreat. His Battalion was trying to cross the Canal D'le Escault when they came under fire from the enemy. Sid was killed in this action. If he was buried, his grave was later lost and he is remembered on the Vis-en-Artois Memorial to the Missing.

It was 99 years later, that Sid's great-great-Niece, Sharon Anthony and her husband Mike paid tribute to him on The Frontline Walk. Sharon takes up the story:

"During his service, Sid kept in contact with his family at home and sent home pieces of trench art. One that remains within the family is a postcard, sent to my grandfather in 1918.

When I was first told Sid's story, I was actually shocked. It was hard to understand how he had joined the RNVR and ended up in the carnage of trench warfare at Gallipoli and the Western Front. Then there was pride, proud of his service and sacrifice, of his award of the Military Medal, which still today is a mystery. Of course, there is the sadness of the loss of a young life, wasted. Sadness for his wife and family, left behind like so many others, to mourn their loss.

Sharon's relative Frederick Driffel killed in the last weeks of the war.

During the coming days, what would surprise us was how emotional the experience would be. The memories and feelings attached to those endless cemeteries and endless white headstones and crosses will stay with me.

Memorial Cross left by Sharon at the Vis-en-Artois Memorial in memory of Frederick.

So we decided to do the walk as we had never visited the battlefields before.

We had trained reasonably well ahead of the walks, so we felt confident about the challenge. But the nerves kicked in as we travelled down to London. But our nerves and worries disappeared when we met fellow walkers at a pre-walk dinner the night before departure and at Wellington Barracks the next morning when the buzz and banter put us back in our comfort zone, reminding us of friendship, camaraderie and support that we had experienced in the army.

We visited the Vis-en-Artois military cemetery where Sid is commemorated on the memorial. During the coming days, what would surprise us was how emotional the experience would be. The memories and feelings attached to those endless cemeteries and endless white headstones and crosses will stay with me. Tears were not uncommon on the journey, especially across the Somme, and the final stage in Ypres.

Physically, it was challenging. Early morning starts whilst still dark, the effort involved walking 30–40km in a day, getting back to the hotel, preparing yourself for the next morning, getting some sleep then dragging your aching legs out of bed to do it again ... and then again. For anyone thinking of doing this event, what you read is true; a fantastic event, for a fantastic cause and you'll make new friendships along the way. And yes, we've signed up for 2019."

The postcard that Frederick sent home shortly before he was killed.

151

Ray Caines: 2019

Ray Caines signed up to complete The Frontline Walk in 2018 but had to pull out at short notice, entering the 2019 Normandy Beaches challenge instead. Ray was hugely disappointed at not being able to walk in the footsteps of his great-uncle Ernest Caines. A regular soldier in 1st Battalion, Royal Warwickshire Regiment, Ernest arrived in France on 22 August 1914 and only four days later on 26 August 1914, took part in the Battle of Le Cateau. Ray asked one of the Charity's researchers to find out what had happened to Ernest.

According to Commonwealth War Graves Commission records he was killed in action on 8 September 1914, although further research suggested that this was highly unlikely. On 8 September 1914, the Battalion Diary showed that the Battalion was located approximately 20 miles east of Paris, nearly 100 miles south west of where he was initially buried.

His burial record states that, after the Battle of Le Cateau, Ernest together with 45 other men was buried by French civilians in what was described as a 'collective grave' or mass grave, in the German Cemetery near the village of Clary, a short distance from Harcourt. Of the 45 men, eight are identified as being from the Royal Warwickshire Regiment, all killed in the battle on 26 August 1914. In 1922, the graves were all exhumed and concentrated in the cemetery at Honnechy. Ernest's remains were identified by his regimental number that was on his boot. The burial officer had written 8 September 1914 on the burial return.

In addition to placing the Battalion nearly 100 miles away, it also records that on 8 September 1914 the Battalion were in reserve and not involved in any action. This clearly casts doubt on the official date of death recorded, as does the fact that if he had been killed on 8 September 1914, then he would have been moved and buried nearly 100 miles behind the German lines at Clary. It is therefore highly likely that the date recorded was a clerical error by the Registration Officer.

If he was killed on 26 August 1914, it means Ernest was on the Western Front for just four days and thus was killed in his first engagement.

Ironically, had Ray been able to do the Last Hundred Day Offensive Walk, he would have been able to visit his great-uncle's grave as it was the afternoon tea stop, on day two. Ray explained:

"I was disappointed to miss out on the 2018 Frontline Walk but am really looking forward to the 2019 challenge. I was very upset, to say the least, to discover Ernest was in France for just a few days before his death. It is even more upsetting to think that his date of death has been wrongly recorded."

An application to change the date of death on Ernest's headstone will be submitted to the Commonwealth War Graves Commission.

Phillipa Calcutt: 2017 / 2018, Sebastian Calcutt: 2018

Corporal Henry Farmer, of the 13th Battalion, Middlesex Regiment was one of those young men who answered Lord Kitchener's 'call to arms', enlisting in September 1914.

Henry participated in many of the major battles during the First World War, Loos, the Somme (where his Battalion suffered 50% casualties in two days), Messines, 3rd Ypres, the 1918 German Spring Offensive and the final Offensives of the War.

He survived all of these famous battles. Until the final one – the final push towards Mons in October 1918. He was killed exactly a month before the Armistice.

Night attack with
phosphorous bombs,
Gondrecourt, August, 1918.

*It felt as though we had reached
back in history to find a family
member who had been missing
but never forgotten by our family.*

In October 2018, one hundred years and one day later, two members of his family broke off from The Frontline Walk to visit his grave and pay their respects. Philippa Callcut and her son Sebastian, had already followed in Henry's footsteps whilst trekking across the Western Front in 2017.

Philippa and Sebastian (and their teddy bear called Alex) made an emotional visit to Henry's grave in St Aubert British Cemetery. He is buried alongside six of his comrades, who also died that day.

Henry was one of those who had been re-buried after the war, as the War Office explained to his wife Alice in an undated letter. A few months after his death, the War Office returned the few personal possessions that had survived; his cap badge, a wallet and two coins. Phillippa recalled her emotions saying:

Having walked in his footsteps Phillippa and Seb were able to visit the grave of Henry Farmer killed in October 1918.

"It felt as though we had reached back in history to find a family member who had been missing but never forgotten by our family. We were extremely privileged to honour him 100 years after his death and it was so poignant to walk with my eldest son, Seb. We made so many friends amongst the Frontline Walkers."

Sebastian also expressed his feelings:

"Pulling up to the small war cemetery I felt excited as I was about to meet a person I had only ever heard about. Even more poignant with the fact it was a 100 years since his death and no family member had ever visited his grave. It was an amazing moment to have that link with someone from the First World War, it made the walk all the more special as you felt you were walking in their boot steps! Doing the walk with my mother was brilliant, someone to share this experience with and tell stories from the war and just talk about life in general as these experience really do bring to light that friends and families truly are the only things that matter."

John Hatchett: 2018

John Hatchett, from Hemel Hempstead, served for 17 years in the Royal Engineers, including tours in Northern Ireland, the Gulf War, and Bosnia. Knowing that John had served in the Army his uncle shared the story of two of John's great-great-uncles who had served during the First World War, cousins, Claude and Frederick Dicker. John takes up the story:

"After reading the advert about The Frontline Walk, I decided to honour my relatives who had served by signing up and raising money for The Soldiers' Charity. I had been out of the Army for 18 years and probably underestimated the physical effort involved in a 100km walk. When I told my sister Julie that I was going to sign up she said she would do it as well.

Opposite: The weather was not always kind.

Right: Red Cross first aid station, 1918.

The walk itself was both physically and emotionally demanding. When you hear about the scale of the losses it is just a number and it is only when I saw the row upon row of headstones that it really hit home just how many soldiers died on the Western Front. In each cemetery I paid my respects to each and every fallen Sapper I could find and any soldier from Claude or Frederick's Regiments. The scale of the losses and the way the historians on the walk brought to life the stories of the individuals and the battles made me realise how different the battles they fought were over anything I had seen during my service.

What kept me walking on through the pain of swollen feet was the fact those soldiers who footsteps we were following had, by comparison, very poor equipment, only very basic rations and couldn't just stop if they were tired or in pain. They had no hotel bed to go back to at night and they didn't know when it would all end.

The camaraderie of the fellow walkers reminded me of my time in the army. You would always support your friends and comrades, you worked as a team, you supported and encouraged people struggling, and at the end of the day you had a laugh about things even when you were in pain."

Claude and his cousin Frederick died just a couple of miles and three days apart in 1917. Both are still missing and are remembered on the Menin Gate Memorial. John and Julie plan to visit Ypres and pay their respects to their cousins, where they fell during the Battle of Passchendaele; Claude with the 10th Battalion, Royal Irish Rifles on the Pilckem Ridge and Frederick with 4th Battalion, Royal Fusiliers on the notorious Menin Road.

Below: Medal Index Card of C.W. Dicker.

Bottom: British War and Victory Medals as awarded to C.W. Dicker.

Martin Howard: 2014 / 2018

Chartered Surveyor Martin Howard from Shropshire was inspired to take part in The Frontline Walk in 2014, after discovering a personal diary that his grandfather Albert, kept during the war. Martin takes up the story:

"For me The Frontline Walk in 2014 started on the 60th anniversary of the death of my grandfather, Albert Howard, who served with the 10th (Liverpool Scottish) Battalion Kings Liverpool Regiment. He would survive the First World War, being severely wounded in a night assault in Belgium in September 1917. He sadly passed away only six months after retirement from his civilian career.

On that 60th anniversary I was given a black moleskin diary, in which Albert recorded his days of service at the front. Albert recorded the humour, boredom, sadness, horror and the utter terror that young men were thrown into.

In May 2014, my father (Albert's son) and I visited the battlefields. Four weeks after returning I was one of the first to sign up to The Frontline Walk, urged on by my family members.

The 2014 walk was a very personal and emotional journey for me, for many reasons. Along the way I remembered men of the Kings Liverpool Regiment, raised a great sum of money for the charity and forged new and lasting friendships."

The following is an extract from the diary he kept whilst serving in France:

"12 August 1916: Very tired after no sleep for 48 hours. Hard work overnight and heavy shelling. At 7am moved up to line, had a rough passage all day. Got orders at 4pm that we were going over the top at 5.15pm. A Coy men all ready for the job and awaiting order to go. Fierce bombardment commences at 4.30pm one can hardly live under the circumstances. Order to go at 5.15pm boys all over, they are falling on either side, under terrific machine gun, artillery and sniper fire. Heart breaking to see the boys going down. Just 20 yards from wire when I got blown up by shell and was buried. Lucky escape got fear of God for a while. Lay until it went dusk then cleared myself and made for shell hole, while crawling along got two bullets through my haversack, one right through my iron rations.

Saw Morris get hit and went out to dress his wounds under fire, terrible sight he was hit right behind the eyes, both were bulging out. Left him and went for stretcher. On my way back came across B Evans, Eaton and Jackson all wounded. Have not seen Eric Hughes since morning, heard he went over as a batman. Got into trenches at 1.30am much shaken up, the Company had sustained heavy losses. T. Horrocks left out wounded and a lot of the old boys gone. I could only find a dozen of A Company left."

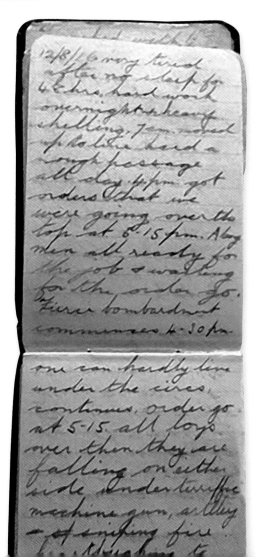

Darren Keightley: 2018

Darren served in the 2nd Battalion, The Royal Anglian Regiment for six years including a tour in Iraq.

> *"My tour of Iraq was the turning point for me, it was an unpopular and un-winnable war. I had two friends from my platoon killed by a roadside bomb while on patrol in a snatch "armoured" land rover which offered little to no protection at all from IED's. It was also a tour that saw me deal with casualties that unfortunately died. My whole outlook on life changed after that tour and I now know how precious life is and how easy it can be unwillingly taken away."*

It was only after his grandfather had died that he discovered an incredible coincidence. He was given a small tin full of photographs. Several showed his grandfather's father-in-law, Private William Sharp, serving in what was then called Mesopotamia (now Iraq) during the First World War. Darren then realised he had followed in the footsteps of William, nearly 100 years later. This revelation inspired him to research his family history and he made a New Year resolution to visit the Western Front and complete a charity challenge. Within ten minutes he had signed up to The Frontline Walk – *"it was a no-brainer"* explained Darren:

> *"My regiment was formed from the Lincolnshire, Northamptonshire, Leicestershire, Bedfordshire, Hertfordshire, Norfolk, Suffolk and Essex regiments. All those regiments were involved in the last 100 days of the war, so I would be following in their footsteps too."*

At one of the cemeteries on the route, Darren proudly wore his regimental beret whilst paying his respects. He explained why:

> *"I never really knew the full scale of the loss of life during the First World War and I was truly taken back when we visited the Arras Memorial. The walls engraved with the names of so many young men, who have no known grave, hit home. I noticed so many graves of fallen soldiers from regiments linked to mine, Northants, Essex, and Leicestershire to name a few. The ages of the fallen reminded me of*

The ages of the fallen reminded me of how young I was when I served in war and the ages of my friends who were killed.

how young I was when I served in war and the ages of my friends who were killed, 19 and 25. What struck me the most was the dates that some of these young men and women died, dying just hours before the guns falling silent on the 11th November or the days after.

I walked around the cemeteries and I noticed the eerie deafening silence of nothing, but 100 years before I could only imagine the sheer chaos and brutality that scarred the area."

Darren discovered that he had four family members who were killed in action on the Western Front, and The Frontline Walk was a fitting way to remember them and his two colleagues who were also killed.

James Liggins: 2018

Although James Liggins' grandfather, Bert Liggins, had served at Contalmaison during the Battle of the Somme in July 1916, it was the fact that he had served at Mons and the subsequent Retreat in August 1914 that inspired James to take part in The Hundred Days Offensive. Bert Liggins served with 1st Battalion, Northamptonshire Regiment [1 Nothants], from 1912 to 1916.

James remembered being told that his grandfather had a finger missing, and he wanted to find out what happened to him. Before embarking on The Hundred Days Offensive, James discovered his grandfather's service record and was able to piece together the story.

In August 1912, Bert joined the Northamptonshire Regiment claiming to be 17 years old. He was in fact just 13 and therefore a 'boy soldier'. In May 1913 he was in hospital for nine days suffering from 'Cowpox'.

The 'Service and Casualty Form' revealed that he arrived in France with his Battalion on 12 August 1914. On 23 August 1914, the German Army attacked the BEF at Mons. Although not directly involved in the battle, 1 Northants' was ordered north to help stem the advance of the German Army from Mons into Northern France and towards Paris. Bert and his comrades took part in the retreat from Mons south to the River Marne where the German advance towards Paris was finally halted. The Germans then withdrew north towards the river Aisne where they dug in and waited. The British then made several attempts to cross the River Aisne and push the Germans back from the high ground. It was during the Battle of the Aisne on 13 September 1914 that Bert was wounded, suffering a shrapnel wound to his right hand. He was evacuated back to England to recover. At the start of day three of the Hundred Days Offensive walk, James found that he was very close to where Bert had been on 24 August 1914.

Bert returned to France on 25 September 1915 and re-joined his Battalion. On 1 July 1916 the Battle of the Somme started and one week later on 7 July 1916, 1 Northants, moved up to the frontline and into the German trenches that had been captured on 2 July 1916 at Fricourt.

The next day they attacked the village of Contalmaison – 31 members of the Battalion were killed and such was the ferocity of the fighting that only one of the bodies has an identified burial. The remainder are still missing and are now remembered on the Thiepval Memorial to the Missing. It was during this action that Bert was wounded again.

In July and September 1918 he was in trouble for missing a parade and refusing to obey an order but was discharged in 1919. He returned home and married Jane in 1924. He died at the relatively young age of 49 in 1948, before James was born.

The next day they attacked the village of Contalmaison – 31 members of the Battalion were killed and such was the ferocity of the fighting that only one of the bodies has an identified burial.

Walkers on the Western Front Walk passing through Contalmaison where James's grandfather fought in 1916.

Iain Lindsay: 2018

Former Royal Marine Iain Lindsay wanted to commemorate the 100th anniversary of the end of The First World War. His grandfather, Harold Lindsay, had survived the war; when he died in 1990, he left behind his diary which helped Iain understand what it must have been like for Harold and his comrades. Iain takes up the story:

"Grandad's ambition was to join the cavalry as he had been used to horses all his life. In October 1915 he went to a recruitment office in Derby where he saw someone dressed in riding garb. He found out he was a Royal Field Artillery Sergeant who persuaded him to 'Join our mob, you'll get more fun than the cavalry.' They were not recruiting. He wondered aimlessly through town questioning, 'Why appeal for recruits?' He saw a sign for another recruitment office that was asking for men for the Royal Garrison Artillery. On 5 November 1915 he returned with two references and was sent to Normanton Barracks. The clerk gave him a look when he told him his age which he instantly upped to 19. Still not satisfied the clerk queried what his year of birth was to which grandad replied '1896'. 'Satisfying the doctor, I took the oath, accepted the "King's Shilling", and became a pawn in the greatest game ever played'."

Gunner Harold Lindsay, Iain's grandfather, who survived the war.

The following excerpts are from a chapter he titled '*The Retreat*' and relates to the German Spring Offensive on the Somme in March 1918:

"As the falling shells thickened, so our pace quickened. This did not lessen the danger at all, for a galloping horse is just as likely to be hit …

The high explosive shells bursting around in rending crashes helped us to a quick decision. Knowing our team, I headed my horses for the steep outlet. If there were any contrary orders shouted at me I failed to hear them in the confusion.

Barely had we moved when the roadway where we had limbered up was blown in all directions. A near one, but no damage to us.

The crashing of the shells, set our team off at a gallop ... no team could have maintained that pace ... we checked from a gallop to a trot, and as the gradient grew steeper ... to a walk. It was terror that kept those poor horses going. Sobbing and gasping for breath, they struggled along.

The top was reached at last. Ours was the first gun out. A few yards on the level took the edge off the distress of the horses, then with a down gradient ... our speed grew to a canter again. None of the shell holes in the road were big enough to cause us much inconvenience ... Our sole object was to get out of that hell. Our troops had a knack of giving fitting names to certain parts of the line, but I think none had a more appropriate name than 'Death Valley' for it was a veritable death trap."

Andrew Volans: 2016 / 2018

Having completed The Frontline Walk in 2016, Andrew Volans from Chepstow decided to take part in The Hundred Days Offensive in memory of his wife's ancestor, Herbert Pollington, 3rd Battalion, Grenadier Guards. To make life harder for himself on the cobbled roads of northern France, Andrew opted to complete the walk in full First World War RAMC uniform! He takes up the story:

"Both of my grandfathers and my great-uncle served; all survived but I never met them. When I met my future mother-in-law I found she had a Princess Mary Chocolate tin containing photos and letter about her great-uncle. I took those and the family stories as a challenge and researched Herbert's service life. We knew he had won the Military Medal and had been involved in a fight at a slag heap. I wanted to understand his experience. The 2018 walk followed in his footsteps at Cambrai and the final offensive which he was part of."

In September 1916, he took part in the assault at Ginchy on the Somme, and although shot in the buttock he was able to rescue his officer Lieutenant Cornish under fire. He was subsequently awarded the Military Medal for bravery.

THESE ALL DIED IN FAI

An early start; dawn at
the Cambrai Memorial.

*I wanted to understand Herbert's
experience. The 2018 walk followed
in his footsteps at Cambrai and the
final offensive which he was part of.*

At the Cambrai Memorial, Louverval before dawn on day one.

Above right:
Guardsman Herbert
Pollington in whose
memory Andrew
walked.

Following a period of recovery in the
UK, by November 1917, Herbert was back
on the battlefield near Cambrai. He was
involved in actions near Flesquieres,
Bourlon Wood and in the Guards Division
assault on Fontaine Notre Dame. On day
one of the Walk, Andrew walked along
the same route followed by Herbert 101
years earlier.

On 27 September 1918 the Guards
Division returned to the area, assaulting
the Canal Du Nord and the Hindenburg
Line. Herbert was mentioned in the
Battalion Diary as taking a defence position
known as the 'slag heap', situated on
the bank of the canal. As the last of the
German prisoners were sent back to the British lines, one turned
and threw a grenade. The diary had therefore confirmed the family
story that Andrew had been told. The first days route crossed
the canal at the very point where this fight had taken place.

Sadly, Herbert's story had a tragic, but very brave ending.
After the Armistice, Herbert was sent to Cologne with the Army
of Occupation. On 31 January 1919, the troops were skating on

Andrew in the uniform of an officer of
the Royal Army Medical Corps.

the frozen River Rhine when four German children fell through
the ice. Herbert jumped into the water and successfully rescued
them but drowned in the process of saving the last child in the
icy water. He was buried with full military honours in Cologne
Southern Cemetery.

A newspaper report stated that Herbert had been wounded
six times, gassed twice and also shell-shocked. His bravery
wasn't just confined to the battlefield. Four families were, no
doubt, forever grateful to him for saving their children all those
years ago.

The letter from Rev.
Phillimore recording
the death of Herbert
Pollington.

Feb. 4. 1919.

Dear Mrs Pollington,

I believe Sergeant Harrison of the 3rd Batt. Grenadier Guards,
has written to you, with regard to the sad death of your son,
Herbert Pollington, by drowning.

It happened on the 31st of January, when I know myself, what
the state of the ice was. It was po...   ...skate on, but was on
the thin side. The Doctor and I had
...hour of the beforehand.

Your boy apparently saw so...
the ice. Your boy had his skates...
succeeded in saving several chil...
3 and 4. It is hard when you do...
in the final attempt to save the...
Whether it was cramp or what, I k...
came back to our barracks, close...
in, but it was too late; he had...

He was brought back to the...
today. There were, I am sure,...
including one from the Mayor of...
at the funeral. We had the dr...
again at the Cemetery. He is...
which is on the northern outsk...
really a very beautiful Cemet...

The Last Post was played...
March, and the firing party...

Now, with regard to your boy, what can I say?
As you know, I daresay, he was one of the bravest of the brave.
He was quite one of the finest lads I have ever seen. He was the
first English soldier in Maubenege, when his Batt. took it.
He was the first with his Officer, Mr Gibbon, to take Slag Heap,
a strong machine gun position, on the 27th of September last.
He was always ready for anything, and I can tell you this, that
...in his Regiment. He was universally beloved by all who knew him
and he has a very wide circle of friends.

God bless you, and know for sure, that your boy was one of
the finest lads that ever breathed, and this act of self-sacrifice
at the end, was the crowning feature of his life.

I am sending you a cheque for the money I found in his pocket.
I am also sending on other effects whilst the Company will send on
the rest.

God be with you.

Yours Sincerely,

CHAPLAIN.

173

Michael Walsh: 2018

In February 2018, former soldier Michael Walsh was sitting in his office in Derby and thinking about the challenge of The Frontline Walk, then still six months away. He had always known that his great-grandfather, Edward Bentley, had died in the First World War whilst serving in the Manchester Regiment. But he didn't know what had happened to him. Until that day, when he received a research document from one of the charity's researchers.

Michael is not afraid to explain how he felt that day:

"I sat at my desk in the office and was reduced to tears when I read the file. We had been looking for him for so long and it was so special to finally discover what happened to Edward. It was even more special to see a letter to the war office written in my great-grandmother's own handwriting."

Edward was reported as *"missing – presumed dead"* during an attack on Trones Wood during the Battle of the Somme in July 1916. His body was never found, and he is commemorated on the Thiepval Memorial to the Missing.

Michael originally signed up for the walk with a friend who dropped out. He met two other walkers though and completed his training with them before setting out for The Hundred Days Offensive. Michael suffered an early injury during the three day walk:

Michael's great-grandfather Edward Bentley was killed on the Somme in 1916 and his name is recorded on the Thiepval Memorial.

Left: The traditional group photograph at the end of the walk.

Below left: Emotions spill over.

"I pulled a leg muscle on the first day and the pain was horrible but I managed to finish with help from the medics. By day three I was in so much pain but was determined to get to St Symphorien Cemetery, which was the end of the walk. I entered the cemetery on the shoulder of a fellow walker with tears of joy and sadness. I was sad because I had made so many new friends who had helped each other throughout the challenge and we were now going our separate ways. But I was happy because we had raised funds for the many who still need our help."

ABF THE SOLDIERS' CHARITY TODAY AND BEYOND

2017/18

- The charity's total charitable expenditure was around £17.3m, ensuring a complete spectrum of support to more than 70,000 members of the Army family. This includes a £7.1m grant to the Defence and National Rehabilitation Centre – the largest in their 75 year history

- The charity has supported the British Army family all over the world – in 68 countries last year

- The youngest person they supported was two years old, the eldest was 102

- The charity funded 92 other charities and organisations that are providing specialist support to the Army family

- The charity awarded £3.7m as grants to individuals in need

- The charity was named as Britain's Most Trusted Charity by Third Sector, jointly with The Royal British Legion

Above: World War Two veteran Sid Sallis is the last surviving RASC Air Despatcher to serve during the Battle of Arnhem in 1944. The charity awards Sid an annual grant towards his care home fees.

Opposite: Charity beneficiaries Charles Louis, Karly Bond, Mark Stevens, Andy Reid and Bob Semple, pictured in 2019.

Left: At the Arras Memorial.

Below: Another day and more respects to pay.

The Frontline Walk is an amazing, emotional event. Everyone works as a team and you feel part of a much larger family.

If you have been inspired by the stories in this book, or are interested in finding out more about either the charity or its events programme, visit **www.soldierscharity.org**.

LIST OF PARTICIPANTS

The list of participants also includes Charity staff highlighted in Red and Classic Challenge staff in Blue. Although they are responsible for the running of the walk, with the exception of those on support vehicles, the rest of the support team completes the walk alongside the fundraisers.

Abi Davies 2018
Adam Wood 2016
Adrian Carter 2018
Adrian Smith 2018
Alan Gillanders 2016, 2018
Alec Barrs 2018
Alexander Gaddes 2015, 2017, 2018
Alicia Riley 2017
Alison Abrahams 2014, 2015, 2016, 2017, 2018
Alison Ratcliffe 2018
Alister Walker 2018
Amy Kenyon 2014, 2015, 2016, 2017, 2018
Andrew Bish 2017
Andrew Courtney 2017
Andrew Garthwaite 2017
Andrew Harris 2017
Andrew Hastings 2018
Andrew Main 2016, 2018
Andrew May 2018
Andrew Perriman 2017
Andrew Volans 2016, 2018
Andy Herrick 2016, 2017, 2018
Andy Price 2016, 2018
Andy Raeburn 2017

Angela Postill 2015
Anne Barrett 2017
Ann-Marie Jefferys 2016, 2018
Anthony Benham 2015, 2017, 2018
Antony Preston 2014, 2016, 2017
Ashley Watson 2018

Barbara Hocking 2017
Barry Groves 2018
Becky Harrison 2018
Ben Gray 2018
Ben Hodges 2014
Bernard Brown 2018
Beth Moos 2017, 2018
Bettina Mankowski 2018
Bill Rowlands 2018
Bob Ruddick 2015
Bonnie Roberts 2018
Bris Lightowler 2018
Bruce Leslie 2018

Camilla Cornock 2016
Cara Wallace 2018
Carol Bratcher 2018
Carol Williams 2016, 2018
Cath Rhodes 2015, 2017

Catharina Johnson 2017
Catherine Edwards 2017
Ceri Sudron 2017
Charlene McIntosh 2017
Charles Taylor 2016
Charlotte Ann Catherine Ward 2015
Cherie Bell 2016, 2018
Chris Byrne 2018
Chris Chapman 2016
Chris Grice 2018
Chris McIntosh 2014
Chris Mirzai 2014, 2015
Chris Mullane 2017
Chris Price 2017, 2018
Chris Woolsey 2017, 2018
Christian Ashdown 2015
Christine Evans 2015
Christopher Coakley 2018
Christopher Green 2018
Christopher Havelock-Davies 2016
Christopher James Collins 2015
Claire Gray 2018
Clare Crouch 2016, 2018
Claude Fallik 2015, 2016, 2017, 2018
Colin Beesley 2015, 2016, 2017, 2018

Colin Freeman 2015, 2018
Colin Greenwood 2018
Craig Evans 2015, 2016, 2017, 2018
Dan Turnbull 2018
Daniel De Bond 2018
Daniel Mortimer 2016
Daniel Ratcliffe 2017
Daniel Tanner 2014
Danny Brady 2018
Darren Aitchison 2015
Darren Keightley 2018
Darren Parker 2017
Darren Slade 2017
Dave Wills 2016, 2018
David Abercrombie 2017, 2018
David Brown 2018
David Buckley 2018
David Cole 2017
David Guild 2016
David Hampton-Davies 2017
David Jefferys 2018
David Jones 2018
David Keen 2016
David Lawson-Evans 2018
David Leslie 2017
David McKenna 2016
David Norton 2018
David Sharp 2018
David Taylor 2018
David Warren 2016, 2018
Dean Gough 2017
Dean Port 2017, 2018
Derek Price 2018

Ed Smith 2016, 2017, 2018
Eddie Strausa 2018
Elly Clark 2016, 2018
Emma Kramer 2017

Finbar Willis 2017

Gareth Beck 2015
Gareth Benn-Edwards 2017
Garry Crawforth 2015
Gary Rhodes 2016
Gary Sadler 2017
Gavin Kramer 2015, 2017, 2018
Gideon Seligman 2016, 2017, 2018
Gillian Green 2017
Godfrey Morris 2015
Gordon Brown 2017
Graeme Wigglesworth 2016
Graham Harris 2017
Graham Mutch 2016
Graham White 2018
Guy Parker 2017
Guy Sudron 2015, 2017

Harry MacLean 2015
Heather Perry 2017
Heidi Maidment 2016
Heidi Went 2018
Helen McMahon 2016, 2017, 2018
Helen Nall 2016
Helen Robertshaw 2018
Helen Seims 2014, 2016, 2018
Henri Stewart 2014, 2015, 2016,
    2017, 2018
Henry Price 2016
Hugh Mcnulty 2018
Huw Edwards 2018

Iain Cassidy 2018
Iain Lindsay 2018
Ian Beach 2018
Ian Houghton 2015
Ian Hughes 2016, 2018

Ian Johnstone 2014
Ian Mason 2016, 2018
Irwin Edgar 2017, 2018

Jackie Bird 2018
Jaime Parker 2015
Jake Preece 2017
James Harcus 2016
James Liggins 2018
James McLoughlin 2015
James Stewart-Smith 2016
Jamie Halliday 2018
Jamie Smith 2016
Jane Hilder 2018
Jane Stevens 2017
Jane Tutte 2016, 2018
Jane Verlaan 2018
Janine Pirrie 2016
Jason Sherer 2018
Jean Peasley 2018
Jenn Whitehorn 2018
Jennifer Baulk 2016
Jeremy Dyer 2016
Jessica Roper 2018
Jimmy (James) Fowles 2015
Jo Richardson 2018
Jody Gorham 2018
John Aitken 2018
John Barr 2016, 2018
John Cavana 2016, 2018
John Cockburn 2017, 2018
John Fitzgerald 2017
John Hallows 2017
John Hatchett 2018
John Hymas 2017
John Jeffs 2017
John King 2018
John Little 2016, 2018

John Mckeown 2018
John McKnight 2015
John O'Connell 2015
John Preece 2017
John wright 2017
Johnny Halliday 2014
Jon Asquith 2018
Jon Griffiths 2018
Jonathan Benn 2018
Jonathan Hornagold 2015
Jonny Peat 2018
Josh Griffiths 2014
Josh Heugh 2014
Judith Tetlow 2018
Julian Bromley 2018
Julian Hammond 2017
Julie Adolph 2018
Julie Riley 2017
Justin White 2018

Karen Cracknell 2017
Karen Routledge 2016
Karen Windmill 2016
Kate Marshall 2016
Kate Metcalfe 2014
Keith Sharp 2015, 2016, 2017
Keith Sherer 2018
Ken Robinson 2015
Kenneth Creek 2015
Kenneth Yardley 2016
Kevin Gorman 2014
Kevin Wenderott 2015
Kira Leith-Ross 2016
Kirsty Irvine 2014
Kirsty Laird 2015, 2017
Kit Harden 2015

Laura Bowkett 2016
Lee Hewitt 2015

Lee McKay 2015, 2016, 2018
Leslie Stoddart 2017
Lewis Macdonald 2018
Linda Cannon 2017
Lionel Henry 2016, 2018
Lisa Blewitt 2016, 2018
Lisa Hamilton-James 2018
Lou Grew 2015
Louise O'Connell 2016
Louise Robiati 2016
Lucy Betteridge-Dyson 2016
Lucy Thomas 2016, 2017, 2018
Luke Box 2017
Lynn Downey 2016

Mandy Walmsley 2018
Marcelle Kite 2015, 2017
Maria Mullane 2017
Mark Bryan 2017, 2018
Mark Campbell 2016
Mark Dowle 2015
Mark Dyson 2016
Mark Eccleston 2018
Mark Lloyd 2018
Mark Nolan 2016
Mark Smith 2017
Mark Ward 2018
Markus Liebenberg 2015, 2016, 2017, 2018
Martin Clark-Tunnicliff 2018
Martin Goodwin 2016
Martin Grubb 2018
Martin Howard 2014, 2018
Martin King 2017, 2018
Martin Leighfield 2018
Martin Rogers 2018
Martin Rush 2016
Martin Shepherd 2016, 2018
Martin Walker 2016, 2018

Martyn Bird 2018
Martyn Leader 2018
Mary Lawson-Evans 2016, 2018
Mat Scott 2018
Matt Ladbrook 2016
Matt Moores 2018
Mervyn Albon 2017
Michael Anthony 2017
Michael Connaughton 2018
Michael Standen 2015
Michael Vallance 2014
Michael Walsh 2018
Michelle Spevick 2017
Mickey Pearse 2017

Nathan Brown 2014
Neil Fox 2016
Neil Hallos 2016
Neil Scarff 2017
Neil Springall 2018
Neil Timmins 2016
Nicole Duncan 2017, 2018
Nicole Goodwin 2016
Norma Hunter 2018

Owain Price 2018

Patricia Fitzgerald 2017
Paul Critchley 2016, 2017, 2018
Paul Dunne 2017, 2018
Paul Hodgson 2017, 2018
Paul McCormick 2014
Paul Sansom 2017, 2018
Paul Stevens 2018
Paul Vickers 2018
Paul Worsley 2017
Pauline Tovey 2017, 2018
Peter Chilcott 2016, 2018
Peter Cracknell 2017

Peter Duncan 2017, 2018
Peter Hulme 2017, 2018
Peter Lamb 2014
Peter Lightfoot 2015
Peter Lough 2017, 2018
Peter Love 2014
Peter Moore 2016
Peter Nevill 2016, 2018
Peter Stevenson 2014, 2018
Peter Storer 2015, 2018
Phil Ball 2018
Phil Morris 2015, 2017
Philippa Callcut 2017, 2018

Rachael Lowen 2017
Rachel Grubb 2018
Rachel Herrick 2017, 2018
Ravon Wright 2017
Rhys Williams 2017
Richard Anderson 2016
Richard Barker 2018
Richard Forsyth 2015
Richard Illingworth 2017
Richard Roberts 2018
Richard Taylor 2016
Richard Walton 2016, 2018
Ridley Clayburn 2018
Robert Clarke 2017
Robert Gemmell 2016
Robert Higginson 2015
Robert Hulley 2018
Robert Lawrence 2015
Robert Macrae-Clifton 2016
Robert Matthews 2016
Robert Mitchinson 2016, 2018
Roberto Scalzo 2015
Robin Bacon 2014, 2015, 2016, 2017, 2018
Robin Fox 2017

Rupert Frere 2015
Sam Butler 2018
Sam Dodd 2016
Sandra Patterson 2017, 2018
Sandra Smith 2018
Sara Baines 2018
Sara McCann 2017
Sarah Pylyp 2017
Scott Adams 2015
Sean Price 2018
Sean Whitehurst 2014
Sebastian Callcut 2018
Shane Robinson 2018
Sharon Anthony 2017
Sharon Henley 2014
Sharon King 2018
Shirley Gillanders 2016, 2018
Simon Davies 2016
Simon Diggins 2014
Simon Ford 2017
Simon Last 2014, 2016, 2018
Simon Nethercott 2016
Simon Prior 2015
Simon Raggett 2018
Sophie Coad 2018
Sophy Whyley 2018
Stacey Wood 2018
Stephen Griffiths 2017
Stephen Mockford 2017
Stephen Stubbs 2017
Steve Bish 2017
Steve Marchant 2018
Steve Middleman 2017
Steve Oatley 2014, 2015, 2016, 2017, 2018
Steve Roberts 2016, 2017, 2018
Steven Andrew Milne 2015, 2016, 2018
Steven Hall 2014

Steven Hamlin 2017, 2018
Steven Stanley 2014
Steven Street 2018
Stewart Barnes 2018
Stuart Bigg 2016, 2017, 2018
Stuart Walden 2016
Stuart Wilkie 2016, 2018
Sue Crosby 2016, 2018
Sue Hanson 2018
Sue Mackenzie 2018
Susan King 2017, 2018
Susan Mckeever 2017
Susan Turner 2018
Suzie Ford 2016

Terence Whenham 2014, 2016, 2017, 2018
Terry Varey 2016
Thomas Saunders 2015, 2016, 2018
Tim Brown 2017, 2018
Tim Monk 2015
Timothy Seeley 2014
Tom Cuff-Burnett 2018
Tony Harris 2016
Tony Mottram 2017
Tracey Tripp 2018
Tracy Pitkin 2018

Ursula Griffiths 2018

Vern Littley 2018
Veronica Winter 2016
Victoria Goodall 2018
Vince Morrison 2017
Vivienne Richards 2017

Wendy Glenn 2017, 2018
William Carver 2018

ACKNOWLEDGEMENTS

The Frontline Walk has become a regular event in the annual calendar of ABF The Soldiers' Charity since 2014. It could not however become the success that it has without the efforts of many.

The work of the charity staff and the expertise of Classic Challenge have already been well represented here. But there are numerous others without whose efforts The Frontline Walk simply could not happen. It is not possible here, to name every individual but the following are worthy of special mention for their support over the years.

Firstly to the staff of Wellington Barracks for allowing access to the Barracks where the walkers check in, and gather for the traditional group photograph before heading for the Channel. Secondly to the various coach drivers, without whom we quite simply would not get from A to B.

Without accommodation the event could not happen, and walkers now feel comfortable knowing that they will have a comfortable bed, a hot shower or bath and the opportunity to relax with a drink at the end of each day. Both the Holiday Inn Express in Arras and the Novotel in Ypres have put up with muddy boots and thirsty walkers every October, since 2014. They have also ensured that staff provide an early breakfast on each day and allowed flasks and water bottles to be filled.

There are too many restaurants to mention individually both in Arras, Ypres and in 2018, Mons, but the hot and substantial evening meals provided have allowed walkers to replenish energy supplies.

To the Last Post Association in Ypres, a special thank you for allowing the group to take pride of place across the Menin Gate and for permitting the wreath layers and members of the charity staff to participate in the Ceremony.

Following The Hundred Days Offensive in 2018, a special thank you must go to the French historian, Phillipe Gorezynski, who arranged a special opening of the Cambrai Tank 1917 Museum at Flesquieres to allow visitors the opportunity to visit the British tank 'Deborah' during the morning refreshment break on day one.

Thanks should also go to all the walkers listed in this book. They don't just complete the walk, in itself a physical and an emotional effort, but they also spend hundreds of hours training and raising the funds needed to take part. We would also like to thank the families of these fantastic individuals for supporting them in their endeavours and all those who have supported them through sponsoring their efforts.

Finally we cannot conclude without saying a thank you to all those men who served, and in whose footsteps the walkers tread.

We are grateful for the support of the following companies in the production of this book: MJH Rating Consultancy, Starspeed, HRS Creative, Crystal EV and Idemia.

PHOTO CREDITS

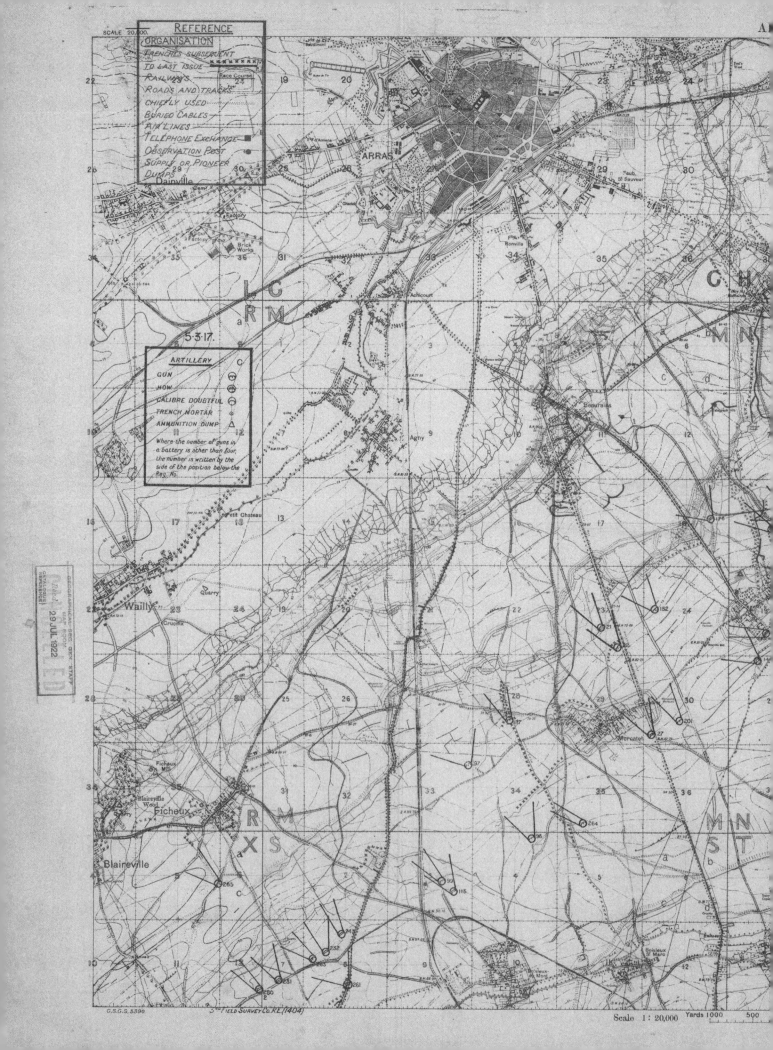

REFERENCE

ORGANISATION
TRENCHES SUBSEQUENT
TO LAST ISSUE
RAILWAYS
ROADS AND TRACKS
CHIEFLY USED
BURIED CABLES
AIR LINES
TELEPHONE EXCHANGE
OBSERVATION POST
SUPPLY OR PIONEER
DUMPS

SCALE 20,000.

5·3·17.

ARTILLERY
GUN
HOW
CALIBRE DOUBTFUL
TRENCH MORTAR
AMMUNITION DUMP

Where the number of guns in
a battery is other than four,
the number is written by the
side of the position below the
Reg. No.

ARRAS

Dainville

Wailly

Ficheux

Blaireville

Mercatel

Agny

Beaurains